The Phaistos Disc and Antikythera Mechanism: The History of the Most Mysterious Artifacts from Ancient Greece

By Charles River Editors

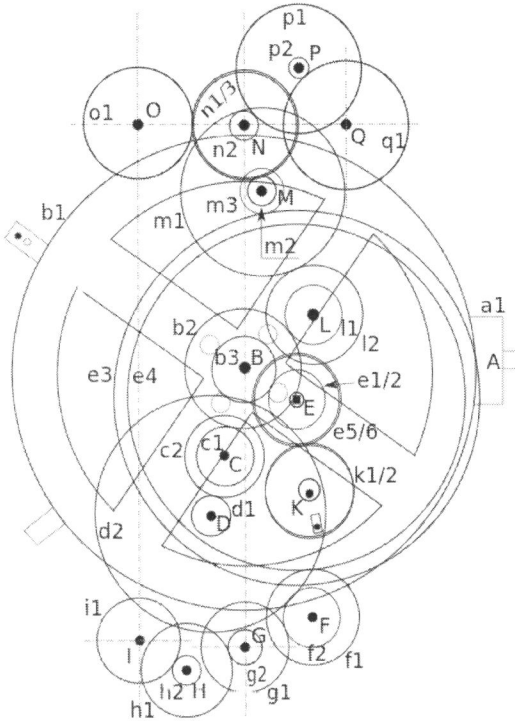

The schematic of the Antikythera Mechanism

About Charles River Editors

Charles River Editors is a boutique digital publishing company, specializing in bringing history back to life with educational and engaging books on a wide range of topics. Keep up to date with our new and free offerings with this 5 second sign up on our weekly mailing list, and visit Our Kindle Author Page to see other recently published Kindle titles.

We make these books for you and always want to know our readers' opinions, so we encourage you to leave reviews and look forward to publishing new and exciting titles each week.

Introduction

The Phaistos Disc

C. Messier's picture of Side B of the Phaistos Disc

The pre-modern world, especially the ancient world, is full of many mysteries, riddles, and enigmas that have perplexed scholars and lay people alike for centuries. One does not have to search long to find some of these mysteries. Ancient Egypt is often thought of as one of the most arcane of all civilizations with many aspects of its culture that are only now coming to light. For instance, the hieroglyphic script was not deciphered until the 19th century and to date scholars are still unsure about the details concerning how the pyramids were built or how mummies were made since there are no extant ancient "guidebooks" of either. In the New World, the sudden decline of the Mayan culture has captured the imagination of many for generations as the Maya left no records detailing their downfall.

Likewise, the oldest European culture to reach the status of "civilization" – the Minoans – remains a mystery to the modern world in many ways. Nearly 2,500 years after the Golden Age of Athens, people across the world today continue to be fascinated by the Ancient Greeks, but the Greeks looked up to the Minoans. In Homer's *Odyssey*, Odysseus makes note of "a great town there, Cnossus, where Minos reigned." It was perhaps the earliest reference to the Minoan civilization, a mysterious ancient civilization that historians and archaeologists still puzzle over, but a civilization that renowned historian Will Durant described as "the first link in the European chain."

Nearly 2,000 years before Homer wrote his epic poems, the Minoan civilization was centered on the island of Crete, a location that required the Minoans to be a regional sea power. And indeed they were, stretching across the Aegean Sea from about 2700-1500 BCE, with trade routes extending all the way to Egypt.

The power of the Minoan civilization and its commercial dominance in the Mediterranean came to an abrupt halt around 1400-1500 BCE. Archeologists have found evidence that many of the Cretan cities suffered severe damage and were ravaged by fire at the same time Minoan trade diminished. Although some of the cities were reoccupied and partially rebuilt, the Minoan civilization never fully recovered. There is evidence that the Myceneans from the mainland began to occupy the cities of Crete and became the dominant traders in the Eastern Mediterranean.

What caused this sudden collapse of the vibrant civilization of the Minoans? Throughout the late 19th century and much of the 20th century, some scholars believed the Minoans were unable to maintain their dominance over the bellicose Myceneans, while others speculated the growth of the Minoan population could not be supported by the agricultural production of Crete. However, recent archaeological finds have led to a consensus among scholars that the Minoan civilization was destroyed by a natural cataclysm. The Greek philosopher Plato, in two of his dialogues, relates a legend concerning the complete destruction of a fabulous city called Atlantis. It was, he said, "swallowed up by the sea and vanished". This tale has intrigued generations of treasure hunters and enthusiasts of mysticism who have taken the legend at face value. It seems increasingly clear, however, that the story of the destruction of Atlantis as told by Plato is one based on fact with the exaggeration attendant on oral tradition.

The Minoans may have been the first link in the "European chain", leading to the Ancient Greeks and beyond, but questions persist over the origins of the civilization, the end of the civilization, and substantial parts of their history, including their religion and buildings. All of this is largely because their written language, known today as "Linear A," remains undeciphered, and among the more enigmatic finds of this truly enigmatic culture was a small disk-shaped object excavated among the ruins of the Minoan city of Phaistos in 1908. The disc, which has since become known simply as the "Phaistos Disc," contains a number of pictographic symbols that were unrecognized by the scholars who first laid eyes on the object and remain unknown in the more than 100 years since. The contents of the Phaistos Disc, like the Minoan language of Linear A, remain unclear, but that is not for lack of trying by a plethora of scholars, some more credible than others. Many different theories have been advanced, but there is still no consensus concerning its origins, or even if it was intended to be writing.

The Antikythera Mechanism

A picture of the salvaged device

Discovering ancient shipwrecks hasn't been a novelty for thousands of years, but when artifacts were salvaged from a Roman shipwreck off the Greek island of Antikythera in 1900, the discovery of one set off one of the great mysteries of antiquity.

When sponge divers investigated the shipwreck, they found the kind of items often associated with such discoveries, including marble statues, pottery, jewelry, and coins, but they also discovered a strange object, the likes of which nobody had ever seen before. Initially assumed to be pieces of rock, it turned out that the item, soon to be dubbed the Antikythera mechanism, consisted of dozens of pieces, many of which had gears. In fact, while scholars quickly deduced that it had an astronomical purpose, many believed the mechanism was too advanced to actually date back to antiquity.

As it turned out, of course, the Antikythera mechanism did date back to the 1st or 2nd century BCE, and as scholars began to more fully comprehend its abilities, fascination over the device grew. In conjunction with the determination that the mechanism was an analog computer of sorts that could predict astronomical phenomena like the positions of stars and eclipses, conjecture over the origins of the device led to theories over what the Romans were going to do with it, and whether the device was created by the Greek genius Archimedes himself. To this day, debate continues over whether there were predecessors to the model, where the astronomical observations that went into creating the model were taken, and whether the ultimate origins of the device might even be Babylonian.

The Phaistos Disc

Discovering the Minoans

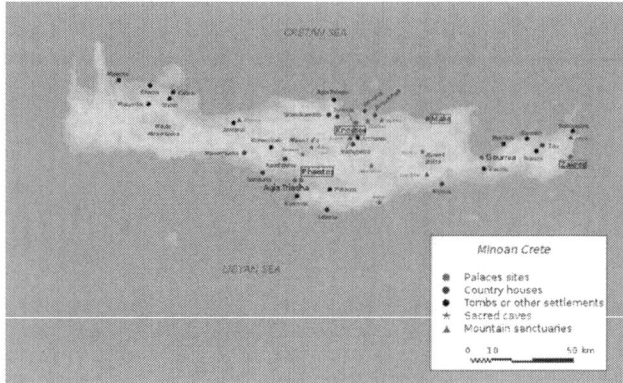

Major Minoan Sites Map: Bibi Saint-Pol

Unlike the civilizations of ancient Egypt, Mesopotamia, and Persia, which were known, if not understood, for centuries due to their long-standing monuments, Minoan culture was only alluded to in the writings of the classical authors and its monuments were all buried under modern settlements in Crete. Still, Minoan culture's one time existence was known by scholars who began to take an interest in discovering it during the 19th century.

The term "Minoan" actually comes from classical Greek sources that stated the legendary King Minos was the first king of Crete. Many of the accounts lack details that could help modern scholars understand the Minoans more, but the fifth century BC Greek historian, Herodotus, wrote some interesting passages about Minos and Minoan Crete. He wrote, "The story goes that Minos went to Sicania – or Sicily, as it is now called – in search of Daedalus, and there met a violent death. . . According to the tradition in Praesus, men of various nationality, but especially Greeks, came to settle in Crete after it was depopulated by the expedition to Sicily; then in the third generation after the death of Minos came the Trojan war, in which the Cretans proved themselves by on means the most despicable champions of Menelaus; their reward for this service on their return home was famine and plague for both mean and cattle, so that for the second time Crete was denuded of its population. This it happens that the present Cretans, together with the remnant of the former population, are the third people to live in the island." (Herodotus, The Histories, VII, 165-171).

Although none of Herodotus's accounts about King Minos or the ethnic mix of early Crete's population can be verified, it plays no small role in the identification of the origins of the

Phaistos Disk. If the ancient Minoan population was as varied as Herodotus' stated, then linguistic origins of the writing on the disk could have originated from a number of different locations.

The 1st century BCE Greek historian, Diodorus, added to Herodotus's passages about King Minos and the Minoans with a few of his own. Although Diodorus' accounts seem to be more focused on mythology, they do relate some of the historical realities of his own time pertaining to the Minoans, particularly that their cities had been long gone by his time. He wrote, "And some say that Daedalus, visiting Egypt and admiring the skill shown in the building, also constructed for Minos, the king of Crete, a labyrinth like the one in Egypt, in which was kept, as the myth relates, the beast called Minotaur. However, the labyrinth in Crete has entirely disappeared, whether it be that some ruler razed it to the ground or that time effaced the work." (Diodorus, Library of History, I, 61).

The labyrinth Diodorus mentions is the one in which the mythological Theseus slew the half-man, half-bull Minotaur. Although the story may have significance concerning Minoan religion in terms of the importance of bulls, the importance of the passage is in the fact that the history and even the cities of the Minoans were for the most part only known to the Greeks in fragments.

There are a few other non-classical, ancient, historical sources that attest to the Minoans' existence. Perhaps the best sources come from the Middle Kingdom of Egypt (ca. 2125-1975 BC) where Minoan vases and other artifacts have been discovered in tombs from the period (Callender 2000, 178). The Minoans, or at least the island of Crete, was also mentioned in some Middle Kingdom hieroglyphic texts where it was referred to as Keftiu (Faulkner 1999, 285). Unfortunately, other than some questionable passages from classical writers and the scant Egyptian evidence, there is little evidence of the Minoan culture outside of the island of Crete.

In the 2,000 years after the decline of the Ancient Greeks, the West was still obsessed with discovering anything related to antiquity that they could, culminating with the discovery of the city of Troy by Heinrich Schliemann in the 1870s. Still, until the end of the 19th century, interest far outpaced findings. Until the 20th century, ideas concerning pre-classical Greece consisted of a few sketchy and wild speculations based on a smattering of looted artworks that appeared on the market. This changed abruptly with the remarkable discoveries of hitherto unknown rich Greek Bronze Age cultures by Schliemann, Arthur Evans and others.

Schliemann

The larger-than-life, amateur archaeologist, Schliemann, was a wealthy industrialist who in his early retirement used his fortune to pursue his belief that the city of Troy, known through Homer's epic poems, was an actual historical place and not, as was commonly believed, a mythical city. Beginning in 1871, at Hisarlik in Turkey, he excavated a large metropolis which he concluded was Homer's Troy. Schliemann published the astonishing results of his excavation *Troja und seine Ruinen (Troy and Its Ruins)* in 1875. He further expanded the knowledge of pre-Classical culture in Greece with excavations, begun in 1876, at Mycenae.

Schliemann will forever be remembered for finding the city associated with the Trojan War and Homer's Iliad, but his findings at Troy were consequential for what it told researchers about the Bronze Age, in the centuries before the Trojan War was presumably fought. In pursuit of further evidence of Greek Bronze Age culture, Schliemann continued to work at Troy, partnered in a dig at Tiryns, and opened up a few trenches at Knossos on the island of Crete. He was prevented from continuing his work at Knossos by inability to acquire the site.

In 1899 the British gentleman scholar, Arthur Evans, acquired a small area of the site at Knossos and began the process of uncovering what turned out to be an extensive Bronze Age city. His excavations continued until 1914, were resumed after the First World War, and continued until 1932. By 1906 Evans had sufficient archeological information to publish a chronology of the Bronze Age culture he discovered at Knossos, which he called Minoan. The name has stuck ever since.

Statue of Evans at the Palace of Knossos

What the people who built Knossos called themselves is still unknown. In Egypt, dating from the period of the rule of Queen Hatshepshut, 1590 - 1550 BCE, there are tomb paintings that show a delegation of individuals presenting tribute, and the individuals are dressed in costumes identical to those seen in the art unearthed at Knossos. Unfortunately, the surviving bits of the image do not name the tribute bearers, although later Egyptian tomb texts refer to a group of people "coming from the shores of Keftiu", a reference to part of Ancient Egypt. Thus, there are no certain links identifying the Keftiu with the people who built the city of Knossos on Crete, Evans's naming of the Minoans has been universally accepted as appropriate, even though it will never accurately explain who the Minoans were.

Before Evans published a detailed description of the excavations at Knossos, books intended for a general audience appeared describing the newly discovered Bronze Age Mycenaean and Minoan cultures of Greece. The entirely new picture of pre-Classical Greece with highly advanced architecture and art intrigued readers who were well acquainted with classical Greek art in museums in Europe and America.

Sir Arthur Evans by William Blake Richmond

In 1909, Evans published the first volume of his *Scripta Minoa: The Written Documents of Minoan Crete*, in which he recorded the texts of inscribed tablets he had discovered at Knossos. In 1921 the first volume of his dig report, *The Palace of Minos*, appeared, and it was followed by four other volumes.

While Evans was concentrating on the rich site of Knossos, other archaeologists were contributing to the quickly expanding knowledge of the now named Minoan civilization. In 1900, German scholar Frederico Halbherr began digging at Phaistos in Crete, eventually uncovering a large Minoan city. Meanwhile, French archaeologist Pierre Demargne worked at a site near Mallia in Crete and in 1901 American Harriet Boyd Hawes began excavating the Minoan city of Gournia, about 40 miles east of Knossos. Hawes brought the exciting discoveries in Crete to the attention of the general public in 1922 in a book she co-authored with husband C.H. Hawes, entitled *Crete, the Forerunner of Greece*. The descriptions in these publications of a civilization which had previously been accessible only to specialists generated worldwide interest and created a new audience for the spectacular discoveries in Crete.

The fascination of the public in Minoan civilization, demonstrated by the throngs of tourists that began to tramp through the several archaeological sites on Crete and through the Heraklion Archaeological Museum, is in large measure a product of two novels by the English writer Mary Renault. As an undergraduate student, Renault became enthralled by the newly discovered civilization revealed by the digs at Knossos while lodging at Oxford University with her relative

Arthur Evans, Keeper of the Ashmolean Museum. She put his scholarly stamp on her extraordinarily popular books, *The King Must Die* (1948) and *The Bull from the Sea* (1969), still widely available in print today.

Renault

The designation of Bronze Age culture in Crete as Minoan was a creation of Arthur Evans. He called the major building he uncovered at Knossos a palace. This palace he identified with King Minos, who was mentioned by Homer in the *Iliad* and *Odyssey*. Homer also says that the craftsman/architect Daedalus constructed a dancing floor or labyrinth on Crete in which the Minotaur, part man part bull, lived. In one of the Greeks' most famous myths, the hero Theseus was challenged to kill the Minotaur. He entered the Labrynth trailing a thread, as he has been told to do by Ariadne, daughter of King Minos and his wife Pasiphaë. Theseus penetrated the labyrinth to the Minotaur's lair, killed him and then followed the thread to escape the architectural trap. The story became expanded in subsequent versions; in Ovid's *Metamorphoses*, Daedalus builds an incredibly complex structure in which King Minos places his wife's son, the Minotaur. The beast was fathered by a white bull that the god Poseidon made the object of Pasiphaë's lust. Fittingly, the Minoans at Knosssos built a palace of such complexity that its structure has been characterized by the adjective labyrinthine.

Ruins of the palace at Knossos

Regardless of whether the naming of the Minoan civilization was accurate or appropriate, Arthur Evans did establish a working chronology of the various levels of Minoan remains at Knossos, identifying Early, Middle and Late Minoan periods. Evans also divided each of these periods into three sub-periods, and in later adjustments to his chronology, the sequence of Minoan civilization has been identified as it is related to the major municipal structure, the palace.

However, not all historians and archaeologists agreed that the large and complex buildings found at many Minoan sites are indeed palaces, so different archaeologists and writers apply different names to the periods in the chronology. Moreover, given that the civilization existed over 4,500 years ago, it should not be surprising that the dates in the following chronology are not firmly fixed, and, as the archaeology of Minoan sites continues, refinements are made to the description of the evolution of Minoan art and architecture. Finally, as with all arbitrary chronologies of ancient and indeed of modern civilizations, it is important to keep in mind that the spread of the Minoans and their existence over the course of a millennium meant their culture did not evolve in a uniform fashion, even though the civilization is all referred to by one name.

In what has been called the Prepalatial Period by some and Early Minoan by others (3000-2000 BCE) the first signs of a post Neolithic Culture or Bronze Age appear in a number of excavated houses. How this culture evolved is unknown. There are at Knossos several levels of Neolithic remains that point to as much as a 3000 year pre-Minoan occupation of the site. The development of ability to create bronze implements not only took considerable time but required the mineral resources of copper and tin that if not found locally could be imported.

In the Protopalatial Period or Early Middle Minoan Period, the old palaces at Knossos, Phaistos and Mallia were constructed, but they were destroyed by an earthquake around 1700 BCE It has been hypothesized by some that after this disaster a people called the Luvians, from south west Anatolia, settled in Crete and brought with them their written language, with a script that has been said to be similar to Linear A, the name given to the first Minoan writing.

The Protopalatial Period was followed by the Neopalatial Period or Late Middle Minoan Period (1700-1600 BCE). The name of the era comes from the fact that new palaces were begun at Knossos and Phaistos. The finest of Minoan decorative art and the finest frescoes in the palaces come from this period. Such was the flourishing of Minoan civilization in this era that some have supposed that Crete became overpopulated.

Fresco at the Palace of Knossos

Like their predecessors, these second palatial structures appear to have been destroyed by earthquake and in some cases consequent fires at the end of this period. The coastal cities of Crete, the harbours and trading centers, were also destroyed.

In the Late Minoan Period (1600-1400 BCE), the Palace at Knossos was partially rebuilt. It is possible that the Mycenaeans from mainland Greece attacked and possibly occupied Knossos, which was then in a very weakened state. Around 1375 BCE, the final palace at Knossos and other palaces in Crete were destroyed by some unknown catastrophe, perhaps more earthquakes or by an invasion of Dorians, the founders of what is now recognized as ancient Greek culture.

Minoan Culture

Fresco of Dancing Women. Photo: Cavorite

If the persuasive (and now possibly predominant) argument among scholars that the great Minoan palaces were religious structures rather than centers of secular royal administration is accurate, then it is clear that religion itself was at the center of Minoan culture. The presence of storerooms, archives, treasuries and crafts workshops in the "palace" complexes, along with the types of decoration and architecture, do indeed indicate that the culture of the Minoans was organized around religion. In the absence of any evidence that Minoan society was structured around a priest king, a position of religious and secular power commonly found in other Bronze Age cultures of the Near East, it is possible that the Minoans were uniquely religiocentric.

A statue from the 7th century BCE that is believed to depict Potnia

The principal Minoan goddess was Potnia, or "The Lady", as she was designated in the inscribed tablets found in the archives of Minoan cities. She is the chief guardian of households and cities, and the primary symbol of Potnia was the double-axe. This kind of axe was called *labrys* in Greek. It is likely that the word, like its cognate labyrinth, made its way into Greek from the language of the Minoans. The double headed axe appears frequently in Minoan temple decoration, in frescoes, and in incised reliefs, and large numbers of bronze symbolic axes have been unearthed.

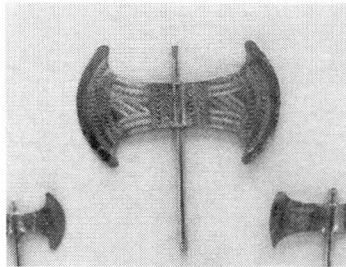

Bronze Double-Axe Ritual Object at the Heraklion Archaeological Museum
Photo: Wolfgang Sauber

Potnia also may have been symbolized by the pillar and the snake, both of which seemed to carry special reverence among the Minoans. At Knossos there is an inscription that records an offering to "Potnia of the Labyrinth", suggesting that a temple to her existed in the "palace" complex.

How Potnia was related to other gods and goddesses in the Minoan pantheon is difficult to determine. Was she the embodiment of all the lesser gods, or did they exist on an equal plane with her? There was a separate deity, or, perhaps just a separate figurative manifestation of Potnia herself, that has been identified as a goddess of fertility and procreation. This deity was represented by a dove. Another goddess or another side of Potnia was the patron of seasonal renewal in nature. Renewal also was assisted by a young male spirit called Velchanos.

Other distinct goddesses who may have evolved over the millennia from various aspects or manifestations of Potnia was the Mistress of Wild Animals, known as Britomartis among the Minoans. Britomartis was also known as the Sweet Virgin, who, it is surmised, evolved into the classical Greek goddess Artemis, the huntress.

Britomartis had a male counterpart called Master of Animals, whose symbols were a shield and spear. It is likely that the cow hide shields depicted in a fresco at Knossos are not military symbols but represent the Master of Animals.

The Minoans not only invoked their gods and goddesses in temples included in the palace complexes of cities, but they also made offerings to them in hilltop and cave shrines, several of which have been excavated in Crete. Briomartis, her male companion, and the goddess of childbirth Eleuthia seem to have been particularly venerated in these remote shrines.

The Minoan universal spirit, Potnia, manifested herself also as a tree goddess. In this guise she was venerated at pillar and tree shrines found in all the major Minoan cities. Further she appears as a Snake Goddess, a deity of the underworld, in artworks unearthed at Knossos where she brandishes snakes in her out-held hands.

From frescoes, seals and other artworks it is clear that religious ceremonies involved dance, and it is assumed that priestesses in these dances first impersonated a goddess and then came to assume a role in which they were considered actual incarnations of the divinities. One of the many religious ceremonies of the Minoans that has captivated archaeologists, scholars and the general public is bull leaping. This acrobatic and possibly dangerous way of honoring the divine has been the subject of considerable speculation.

In the central court of Minoan cities, young athletes (perhaps female as well as male), performed some kind of spectacular dance with a bull. Several interpretations of the bull-leaping ceremony have been put forward based on the depiction of the ceremony in Minoan art, particularly on several seals, some metalwork, and a fresco at Knossos. Evans believed that the leapers grasped the bull's horns and vaulted and summersaulted over the bulls back to land upright either on the back of the bull or on the ground by its tail. Some have argued that this feat of athleticism would've been nearly impossible, and that what the Minoans did was more like modern Spanish bull fighting. Whatever the truth of the matter is, bull-leaping offers a fascinating glimpse of Minoan worship, and it suggests that the Minoans combined sport, dance, and athleticism as part of their religious ceremonies. That combination is a forerunner to the religious aspect of classical Greek athletic competitions at Olympia, the Olympics. The common use of stylized bull horns in the decoration of Knossos, in particular on the cresting of buildings, were constant reminders of the importance of the bull within the religious precinct of the city.

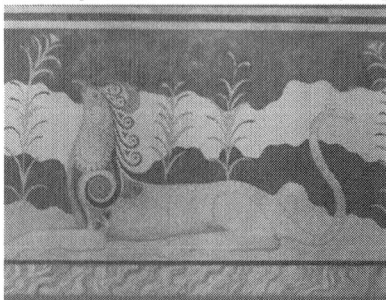

Griffin Fresco in the Throne Room at the Palace of Knossos

Perhaps the most lasting legacy left by the Minoans on the European civilizations that followed them was their art. In Minoan society, the arts and crafts were held in particularly high regard, and it was so apparent during early excavations that the chronology of Minoan civilization is demarcated by the changes in their pottery. Moreover, it seems Minoan art was one of their most valuable trading resources, judging from the findings of Minoan artwork in the ruins of Bronze Age or Helladic Era cities in mainland Greece (part of the Mycenaean Civilization) and the Cyclades and in the Middle East (particularly in Egypt).

Considering the Minoans' capacity to create intricate, beautifully designed art in a variety of ways, all of which demonstrated a highly developed aesthetic and mastery of many often complicated techniques, it is not surprising that they considered art an important, perhaps the most important, avenue in religious expression. In the palaces or temple complexes excavated to date, there are rooms that clearly served as workshops for craftsmen. Remains of looms, bits of carved ivory and pottery shards indicate the that different workshops were dedicated to different crafts of art.

The centrality of art to Minoan culture is also readily obvious in the fact that the buildings at Knossos were brightly colored; Evans even painted his reconstructed columns of the Palace at Knossos red. In the interior spaces, columns shaped like upturned trees that got narrower from the top to bottom were painted and topped by colorful capitals. Ancient Greek columns and the columns that followed got narrower from bottom to top, which is a more practical design in an engineering sense, because columns with a thicker base can support more weight. The fact that the Minoans' columns had it the other way around suggests their purpose was not simply for practical engineering. The columns supported brightly painted ceiling beams that divided the intricately patterned wooden ceiling into squares and rectangles, a kind of colorful decoration that was repeated both inside the buildings and outside.

The walls of some of the rooms were decorated with large frescoes, with such themes as stylized griffins in the so -called Throne Room, and elsewhere with pictures of ritual dancers, bull leapers and dolphins swimming in the sea. The skill of the Minoan painters is not only clearly evident in their careful composition of the scenes and their pleasing use of line and color but also in the technique of their execution - true fresco. The painters worked on wet plaster applied to the stone walls of the rooms. This required quick painting, before the plaster dried, and thus precise planning of each image must have been undertaken before work could begin.

The same sense of form and design and technical expertise is evident in Minoan pottery painting. Patterns, birds, fish and other animals were depicted on Minoan pots in such a way as to utilize the form of the pottery to enhance the impact of the decoration. Some have considered the apogee of Minoan pottery painting to be their Marine Style works that are typified by a wonderfully animated octopus that stretches its many arms over a vessel. One of the many treasures of Minoan painting is the Hagia Triada sarcophagus of about 1400 BCE excavated at a villa not far from Phaistos. It shows a procession of people carrying offerings to an altar. The figures are dressed in ceremonial garb are quite lifelike. They are rhythmically dispersed in a frieze that is enclosed in a brightly painted patterned frame.

Pottery dated between 2100-1700 BCE

In addition to painting, the Minoans excelled in ivory and stone carving. An ivory figure of a bull leaper, found at Knossos and dated around 1600 BCE, is a remarkable example of the fragile but elegant work the Minoans were capable of. The survival of Minoan sculpture in ivory is extremely rare, but a few examples still exist, including one of a group of two goddesses and a divine child dating from the 14th century BCE found in mainland Greece at Mycenae. This work showed that the carvers of Crete were capable of creating moving work that captured not only intricate interaction of human figures but even human emotion. Incorporating facial expressions and emotion in art was fully popularized by the Ancient Greeks nearly a millennium later.

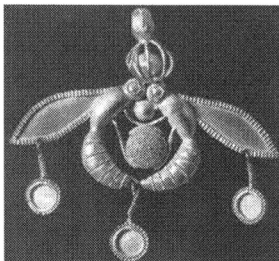

Bee pendant from Mallia

Minoan craftsmen also displayed unusual talent when working with metals. A well known example of their metalwork is an exquisite bee pendant found at Mallia, which dates back to about 1500 BCE In this piece, two bees are arranged facing each other around a honey comb. Their enlarged outstretched wings are decorated with pendants, above their heads is a tiny wire-enclosed ball, and another pendant hangs from where their curved abdomens meet. The artist who made this pendant not only understood the principles of great design; he also had a very good understanding of the form of bees through careful observation of them in nature.

The best known Minoan metalworks are the two Vapheio Cups found in a tomb near Sparta on the Greek mainland. These items were so highly prized by their owner, who acquired them in trade or possibly bought them from a traveling Cretan craftsman, that he had them interred with him so he could enjoy them in the afterlife. The gold cups are decorated with narrative reliefs. On one of the cups, a bull is shown trapped in a net on one side, and on the other side the bull is shown trampling his captors and escaping their clutches. The second cup shows a bull being caught through the use of a decoy cow. The sophisticated reliefs of the Vapheio Cups show that Minoan artists were adept at creating the illusion of space and skilled in recreating the animal's anatomy.

Vapheio Cup

While the examples of artwork in ivory and metal are relatively rare, thankfully the same cannot be said of Minoan seals, of which many existed. The Minoans used seals to ensure security for items of trade. Containers such as the pithoi found in the storerooms in the palaces would be capped and sealed to indicate ownership and to prevent tampering. However, what truly interests observers today is the artwork. Minoan seals can be seen in museums around the world, and they have received considerable attention by scholars. Arthur Evans in particular was drawn to the minute detail of Minoan seal carving.

Seals have been categorized based on their shape, including lentoid, oval, square, and other shapes. The seals were carved from different materials depending on their age, including bone, ivory, steatite, carnelian and agate for earlier seals. In the later Minoan period from 1700 BCE and on, seals were carved from jasper, chalcedony, lapis, hematite, amethyst and obsidian, and the shapes included cylinder, cone, prism or signet ring.

Minoan seals have an unbelievable array of designs that provide a kind of encyclopaedic picture of Minoan society. Motifs include animals, human figures, proto-heraldic designs, symbols and lettering, ships, buildings, goddesses and religious ceremonies. The subjects of Minoan seals are more often than not so carefully rendered that they provide a view of civilization that is unequalled in the ancient world. From these seals comes an excellent picture of what a Minoan ship looked like, what a Minoan hunt was like, how the Minoans worshipped, what the Minoans wore and other aspects of Minoan life.

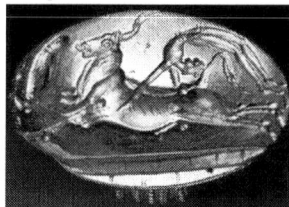

Minoan Seal depicting Bull-Leaping

Palaces and Trade Goods

As archaeologists fanned out across Crete in the early 20th century, they discovered many large settlements built around palaces. Because of this, Minoan culture began to be described as a "palace culture." The most impressive of these sites were located at Knossos, Milia, and Phaistos. Interestingly, the archaeologists quickly learned that the structure of these settlements were very similar, even when the size varied (Preziosi and Hitchcock 1999, 64). From what has been unearthed at these sites, it was discovered that although all contained large palaces, the entirety of the sites were multifunctional in nature. The settlements combined economic, political, ceremonial/religious, and even manufacturing elements. There were some sacred spaces in the settlements that appear to have been off limits to the general public, but the majority of the sites were probably bustling with activity on any given day. In addition to the areas described, the sites of Knossos and Phaistos also had what modern scholars refer to as "theatrical areas," which included a stepped section that would have resembled an early amphitheater (Preziosi and Hitchcock 1999, 64-65). The layout and function of the Minoan palace settlements were unlike the Mycenean citadel palaces or the later Greek temples. If anything, the Minoan palace settlements were more similar to temples in the Near East, but there were significant differences there as well. Truly, the Minoan palace settlements were quite unique in the ancient world.

Based on excavations at Knossos, Zakros, Mallia, Phaistos and Gournia, scholars can confidently assert that Minoan cities were densely packed with houses that lined narrow streets. There were also highly developed water and wastewater systems that ran in a network beneath the surface of the streets.

The large palace or temple complexes were constructed using a variety of building materials. In the interior on the ground floor, the typical building used finely cut gypsum covered with stucco (and in some rooms frescoes). The gypsum blocks were set within a framework of wood beams, which was probably a technique that reduced the damage caused by earthquakes. The floors were of finely polished gypsum and the ceilings were made of wood planks running between large wood beams. The second story was usually constructed with mud brick that was also set in a wood beam framework.

Faience Tablets showing House Facades at Knossos, from the Palace of Knossos

Domestic housing was two or three stories in height, constructed in a similar manner with limestone blocks on the ground floor and mud brick above. A series of faience or glazed earthenware plaques found at Knossos indicates the facades of the urban houses were patterned, which certainly would have given a decorative enhancement to the streetscape.

The organization of Minoan society, and what if any social hierarchies there were, remains unclear. This is largely due to the fact that the first writing system of the Minoans continues to baffle scholars. The language, which has been called Linear A, is found on many of the inscribed tablets unearthed throughout the Minoan world. The second language used by the Minoans, Linear B, was deciphered by Michael Ventris, who discovered in 1952 that the language was an early version of Greek. The texts of the Linear B tablets reveal many details of Minoan life, but without being able to decipher Linear A, some aspects of Minoan life remain in the dark. That said, while the texts of Linear A still baffle scholars, they have given us a clear picture of the

Minoan numerical system. It was a simple decimal system without the use of zero, paralleling that used by the ancient Egyptians.

The layouts of the Minoan palace settlements intrigued scholars, but even more interesting were the items discovered within the sites. Archaeologists were amazed when they found the beautiful frescoes adorning the palace walls that had colorful scenes of men leaping over bulls, bare breasted women, and dolphins swimming in the sea. Interestingly, there is a notable lack of martial scenes in the Minoan frescoes which is a stark contrast from the Minoans' contemporaries in Egypt or Mycenean Greece. In fact, the only weapons so far excavated from any Minoan sites are dated to the Late Minoan Bronze Period (Preziosi and Hitchcock 1999, 17). As magnificent as the frescoes discovered at the Minoan sites are, there were other discoveries that were more important, at least as they pertain to the Phaistos Disc.

As archaeologists uncovered the beautiful frescoes in the palaces, they discovered numerous tablets with an unknown type of writing. At first glance, many scholars thought that the writing was either related to or derived from ancient Egyptian since it was hieroglyphic, but Egyptologists quickly dispelled that theory. Unlike the decipherment of the Egyptian language, which was done through the existence of parallel Greek texts, the Minoan script never appeared alongside any known language. The most scholars could do was guess and give the enigmatic Minoan language and writing a name – "Linear A." It was given the name because the script is written in a linear pattern and the letter "A" because it is the oldest type known to have been used in the Aegean region. Since its discovery over 100 years ago, only about fifty words of the Linear A language have been deciphered, but the language and the tablets themselves remain unreadable (Morritt 2010, 73). Linear A script was used extensively on Crete until about 1450 BCE when the Myceneans conquered the island and replaced it with their own proto-Greek language and script – "Linear B."

The island of Crete is very similar to mainland Greece in many ways in that high mountain ranges and deep valleys made it easier for people in ancient times to travel to other parts of the island by sea rather than land. Also, because of the topography, the Minoans became a sea-based culture which the later Greeks and many scholars have referred to as a "thalassocracy," where the major cities were either located on or near the coastline. The Greeks knew this about the Minoans; the 1st century BCE Greek geographer, Strabo, wrote that "the maritime supremacy of Minos is far-famed" (Strabo, *Geography*, I, 2, 2). Although Phaistos was not located directly on the sea, it did have a nearby harbor which enabled it to be a powerful naval and merchant city.

Minoan economy expanded over the years because they controlled a vast trade network, the full extent of which is not precisely known. However, it is clear from finds in Egyptian tombs and sites elsewhere in the Middle East that the Minoans' sea-empire was incredibly widespread, perhaps stretching from modern Spain to Syria and Egypt. Findings in Egyptian tombs include representations of Minoan vessels in art, particularly on seals, and one appears in an Egyptian tomb painting. The Minoan ships varied in size, from quite modest coastal vessels to larger ships with a mast in the middle supporting a square sail. As many as 15 oars on each side were used to propel the ship on windless days. Some of the art depicts Minoan ships that had high prows and sterns and were steered by a single oar managed from a deck at the stern. The ships are shown with cabins amidship or at the stern. Excavations at Minoan seaports on Crete, at places like Kydonia, Rethymnon, and Amnisos, have also shed some light on Minoan maritime commerce and shipbuilding.

The exact nature and extent of the Minoan empire is not clearly understood at present. There seem to have been colonial cities established around the eastern Mediterranean and on the islands of the Aegean, including Kythera, Naxos, Rhodes, Iasos and Miletus. The relationship between these towns and cities with the cities on Crete is not entirely clear. They may have been vassal city states, or they may have been equal trade partners. The most significant find of a Minoan colony is at Akrotiri on the island of Thera. There were probably Minoan colonies on mainland Greece as well.

The extent of Minoan trading is evidenced by decorative art that has been found in archaeological sites around the Mediterranean. In addition to exporting fine crafts, the Minoans sent timber and woolen cloth to Egypt in exchange for linen and possibly papyrus. It is likely that the Minoans exported surplus olive oil and grain in trade for exotic materials used in the production of luxury goods, such as copper from Sardinia and Etruscan tin from Italy. Tin may even have been imported from as far away as Britain, and there is evidence that some amber found at Knossos may have come from southwest England.

The Minoans also traded their excess wine and olive oil with the Myceneans on mainland Greece and imported a vast array of goods including minerals such as black obsidian from Anatolia, lapis lazuli from Syria (originally brought from Afganistan), and amethyst and carnelian from Egypt. Egyptian beads and scarabs have been found in some Cretan sites as well.

The Discovery of Phaistos and the Phaistos Disc

Olaf Tausch's picture of the palace ruins at Phaistos

Like with many enigmatic aspects of Minoan culture, modern scholars do not know what the Minoans called the city of Phaistos. The name is actually derived from Linear B tablets, which indicates that the city continued to be important into the Late Bronze Age when Crete was dominated by the Myceneans (Preziosi and Hitchcock 1999, 64). Although Phaistos was first built in the Early Minoan Period, it was not until the Middle Minoan Period that it became one of the most important Minoan cities. Scholars believe that Phaistos' importance was derived from its geographic location which was due not only to its location near the southern coastline of Crete, but also because of its proximity to the double-topped Mount Ida (Preziosi and Hitchcock 1999, 65). Modern scholars believe that the mountain held religious significance to the Minoans and that Phaistos was probably a religious center, but because Linear A remains undeciphered, the details of the religion remain unknown. The excavations at Phaistos have not only uncovered the famed Phaistos Disc, but also a settlement and palace complex that rivaled the one in Knossos.

When Italian archaeologist Federico Halbherr first began excavations at Phaistos about 100 years ago, few thought that he would uncover a city that rivaled Evans' discovery at Knossos. The initial excavations discovered a great palace complex like the one in Knossos, but later work at the site revealed that there were actually two palaces, the second was built on the site of the first. The first palace was built in the early Middle Minoan Period while the second palace was built in the Middle Minoan III A-B Period, or sometime after 1700 BCE (Preziosi and Hitchcock 65). It remains unknown if the first palace was destroyed by human hands, was the victim of a natural disaster such as an earthquake or volcano, or was simply renovated. The most likely explanation would be natural disaster since major invasions were not common at that point in the Bronze Age, but anything or a combination of factors could have led to the destruction. Excavations have revealed, though, that the second palace used walls from the first so it may have simply been a renovation or modernization program (Preziosi and Hitchcock 1999, 69). Whatever the reason, it is believed that the first palace was an important social cultural center and also exerted considerable economic influence through its nearby bay and harbor (Preziosi and Hitchcock 1999, 69).

Not long after Halbherr and his Italian team set to work excavating Phaistos and nearby Haghia Triadha, the Phaistos Disc was discovered by Luigi Pernier among the ruins of the Phaistos Palace on July 3, 1908 (Morritt 2010, 94). The disk was part of a cache that included a Linear A tablet dating to Phaistos' first palace, or sometime before 1799 BCE (Preziosi and Hitchcock 1999, 69). The Italian archaeologists were not immediately clear about what they had discovered.

At first, the presence and importance of the Phaistos Disc seemed to have been lost among the general enthusiasm for the much larger discovery of the city itself. It soon became evident that Phaistos's size and importance rivaled Knossos' and the discovery of the disk was just another small part of the overall find. Besides, Linear A had just been identified as a form of writing by Evans so the disk was immediately just thought to be another artifact containing the unreadable language of the Minoans, and it is currently housed in the Archaeological Museum of Heraklion in Crete (Duhoux 2000, 597).

The disk itself is actually fairly small, only eight inches in diameter, and is made of clay. Modern scholars believe that the signs were impressed onto the disk when it was wet in a process similar to that used in Mesopotamia to inscribe the cuneiform script onto clay tablets. The inscriptions, which are on both sides of the disk, are believed now by most scholars to have been read from the outside to the center (Duhoux 2000, 597), but like with nearly every other theory pertaining to the disk, it remains unproven. There are 45 distinct signs on the disk that are used in 61 compartments for a total of 241 tokens (Schwartz 1959, 106). The signs are hieroglyphic in nature – many being representative of humans and animals – but it is unknown if they are to be understood as idiomatic, phonetic, or both. For instance, in the ancient Egyptian hieroglyphic script, certain signs could be both. A slice of bread is often equated to the phonetic value of a "t" sound in modern English, but could be a determinative for "bread" if used at the end of a word. With the Phaistos Disc, there is a sign known as the "crested warrior" because it is a man's head in profile with what appears to be the feathered crest of a warrior's helmet, and it appears the most (a total of 19 times). Among the least common occurring signs, appearing only once on side B, is a head of a bull or a ram.

The second most frequent sign is a bit enigmatic in itself since it is not part of an animal or human. It is a circle with seven dots inside it, which many believe to be a shield, occurring a total of 17 times. Interestingly, the crested warrior is always in what is believed to be the initial position of the word or phrase (Schwartz 1959, 107).

Early Attempts to Decipher the Phaistos Disc

Unfortunately, many of the attempts to decipher the Phaistos Disc border on the absurd and detract from its potential importance as a historical and linguistic artifact. Although most modern scholars of Minoan/Aegean archaeology and history recognize its potential importance, many also view it as somewhat of a distraction; they believe that uncovering the mysteries of Minoan culture will come through the decipherment of Linear A tablets, not the Phaistos Disc. With that said, some of the early attempts to decipher the Phaistos Disc are now an important part of the historiography of Aegean studies.

Since the Phaistos Disc appears to employ a type of hieroglyphic script, some of the first theories regarding its reading centered on a potential Egyptian origin. These theories were quickly discarded by Egyptologists, though, because the ancient Egyptian language had been deciphered for nearly 100 years by the time knowledge of the Phaistos Disc became public. Interestingly, yet absurdly, some scholars also advanced Chinese as a possible origin for the disk (Duhoux 2000, 597). The association of Chinese with the disk proved to be anachronistic because the Phaistos Disc pre-dated writing in China, but led to later theories that the writing on the disk may have been intended to be logographic. Logographic writing, which was employed in early Chinese writing, is a style in which each character represents an entire word. Another far-out hypothesis was that the Phaistos Disc was a form of proto-Basque. Because Basque is a pre-Indo-European language spoken by a small but not inconsequential number of people in the Pyrenes region of southwestern France and north-central Spain, the theory held that the Phaistos Disc was evidence that the language was much more widespread at one time (Duhoux 2000, 597). The theory relied on grammar but failed to account for the fact that Basque was not a written language until the modern period. But not all early attempts to decipher the Phaistos Disc were linguistically orientated; some thought that the disk was actually an astronomical device.

The Phaistos Disc as an astronomical device was first advocated by Leon Pomerance (1976) in a book where he claimed that the Minoans used the disk to plan their planting and harvest cycles based on the position of the constellations Aquila and Serpens. Pomerance listed several points that he believed supported his hypothesis that the disk was astronomical in nature, such as its circular shape. Like many of the more esoteric and some would say bizarre interpretations of the disk, Pomerance used what he believed were parallels in Egyptian history to further his argument. He pointed out that 9 symbols on the Phaistos Disc match with those from the ceiling of the Dendera Temple in Egypt. The relief from the Dendera Temple is an astronomical scene, but it is also apparently closely associated with Egyptian theological ideas. Pomerance also noted that the 61 divisions on the disk could be subdivided into twelve groups, which he thought equated with the 12 months of the calendar. Finally, he thought that the signs on the Phaistos Disc of an eagle and a tail were equated to the constellations Aquila and Serpens.

Although Pomerance's study received some academic recognition in the years after his book was published, it has been for the most part forgotten by Aegean archaeologists. Pomerance's theory operates under many assumptions and most importantly, there have been no later discoveries on Crete that suggest the Minoans had the astronomical knowledge that he claimed.

At the same time, while Pomerance's theory may be on the fringe of academia, it is much more mainstream than other ideas that advocate that the disk is proof of ancient aliens or an antediluvian civilization.

Due to the growth in popularity of alien conspiracy theories during the 1990s, the Phaistos Disc's enigmatic origins began to be viewed as otherworldly, or at least from a forgotten time in this world. Friedhelm Will (2000) and Axel Hausmann (2002) both argued that the Phaistos Disc was proof of Atlantis or some as yet unknown pre-flood civilization. These theories were fun to talk about for many and found some mainstream attention, but were never given serious attention or thought by legitimate scholars.

While the more outlandish theories concerning the language and/or purpose of the Phaistos Disc have garnered some popular attention over the years, especially with the advent of cable television programs that promote the ideas of "ancient aliens" and prediluvian civilizations, more reasonable hypotheses have been the focus of most academics. Perhaps the most logical explanations of the language on the disk are that it is either a variant of Linear A or Linear B. The explanation of course suits the region because Linear A was the writing and language of the Minoans, while Linear B, which is essentially proto-Greek, was used by the Myceneans. Still, since the script on the Phaistos Disc, if indeed it is actually a script, is unlike any known samples of Linear A or Linear B, the classification of it belonging to either of those two languages remains problematic. Schwartz was one of the earliest scholars to assign Linear B to the Phaistos Disc. In his well-thought out articles on the disk, Schwartz deduced that "the writing and syllabary are genetically related to Cretan linear scripts" (Schwartz 1959, 112). Of course, there were two Aegean linear scripts, of which the Phaistos Disc was contemporary with Linear A, but Schwartz deduces that "the frequencies and phonetics with those of the disk yield remarkable coincidences" (Schwartz 1959, 110). Ultimately, Schwartz stated that the language of the Phaistos Disc was probably Indo-European and "the same or similar" to the Linear B used by the Myceneans (Schwartz 1959, 112). Schwartz's arguments, which he detailed in a number of published works, gained acceptance with many in academia during the middle of the 20th century and continued to add adherents for several decades.

Based on Schwartz's work, many scholars of Aegean and classical history decided to attempt a full Greek translation of the disk. Many of these translations resulted in little more than gibberish, but some, thanks largely to creative translating on the part of the scholars, presented a readable text. Paul Muenzer (Muenzer 1985) offered a Greek translation of the Phaistos Disc in a credible yet small academic journal during the 1980s. By the time Muenzer threw his translating hat into the ring, many of the larger journals of classical history, such as *Greece and Rome* and the *Journal of Hellenic Studies*, had been inundated for some time with numerous translations of the Phaistos Disc. Most of these translations were either totally outlandish, gibberish, or simply rehashes of earlier attempts. Because of that, legitimate scholars were often forced to give their translations to lesser known journals. Muenzer believes that the Phaistos Disc was a religious text concerning oracles because "business texts are never made so elaborately" (Muenzer 1985, 271). This assertion may be true if one assumes that the Phaistos Disc was written in a variant of

Linear B, but logic would dictate that it is probably more closely related to Linear A.

Duhoux (2000) is one of the most recent scholars to come out in favor of the Phaistos Disc being related to or a version of Linear A script. Obviously, since Linear A was used by the Minoans and Phaistos was a Minoan city, this would seem to make sense. Of course the problem is that Linear A remains undeciphered which makes positively assigning the inscriptions on the Phaistos Disc unsure. Davis (1970) was one of the first scholars to attempt a Linear A translation of the disk, but the result was a confusing collection of gibberish. More recently, Bowden (1992) also offered a Linear A translation of the disk, but his work too failed to gain traction in academia. Davis and Bowden both believed that the signs on the Phaistos Disc had variable phonetic readings, which resulted in far different translations, and as noted above, gibberish. Without a complete decipherment of Linear A, though, it will be extremely difficult to definitively assign that language to the Phaistos Disc. Although the inscriptions on the Phaistos Disc would most logically seem to be either Linear A or Linear B, there have been some other credible but unproven hypotheses forwarded for other linguistic origins.

During the period when the Phaistos Disc was deposited in the spot where it was eventually discovered in 1908, the Minoans shared the eastern Mediterranean region with the Egyptians to their south and the Hittites to their east in Anatolia. The Hittites employed different styles of writing their language which has led some earlier scholars to suggest that the Phaistos Disc was possibly a form of Hittite. This theory never gained much traction because the only place where the Hittites expanded their empire outside of Anatolia was the Levant and there were no other signs of Hittite material culture in Phaistos. Still, others have suggested that the Phaistos Disc may be Luwian which was an Indo-European language closely related to Hittite (Anthony 2007, 43). Those who forward the Luwian theory point to the number of place names on both sides of the Aegean ending in "anthos" and "assos" as part of the proof that Luwian speakers once inhabited parts of Greece as well as Anatolia. According to this theory, Luwian speaking Indo-Europeans arrived in Greece around 1900 BCE – before the Phaistos Disc was deposited – and were the dominant group until they were replaced by the Myceneans (Macqueen 2003, 34-35). The problem with the Hittite and Luwian theories is that modern scholars can read both of those languages and neither appear to fit the Phaistos Disc.

Finally, other scholars have proposed that the Phaistos Disc has a Semitic language that employed a modified hieroglyphic script. During the period when the Phaistos Disc was made, Akkadian was the most widely used Semitic language and was on its way to becoming a *lingua franca* in the eastern Mediterranean and the Near East. With that said, it would still not be until after 1500 BCE when Akkadian became the diplomatic language of the region, and it was always written in the cuneiform script, not in hieroglyphics. Schwartz's argument that the disk appears to be written in a combination phonetic-idiomatic script would also work against the Semitic argument. He noted that the signs on the disk are "too many for a true alphabet, and too few for a Mesopotamian-Egyptian type syllabary" (Schwartz 1959, 107).

Some Other Considerations on the Phaistos Disc

The biggest problem that modern scholars have had deciphering the Phaistos Disc (and the entire Linear A language and script for that matter) is the absence of a matching disk or text. 19th century scholars were able to finally decipher the enigmatic ancient Egyptian hieroglyphic script when the Rosetta Stone was discovered. The Rosetta Stone contained an accompanying Greek script, which allowed the first translators to "work backwards." Unfortunately, no tablet or inscription has yet to be discovered that contains a Linear A and Linear B text that would allow philologists to likewise work backwards. Although that is yet to happen, an archaeological discovery in Crete appears to confirm that the Phaistos Disc was in fact Minoan in origin.

When Minoan culture was first being unearthed about 100 years ago, an interesting discovery took place near the central Crete town of Arkalochori. Local residents found a large number of bronze weapons in a cave near the town which has since been named the "Arkalochori cave." The weapons were dated to the Late Minoan Period which took place around the time the Myceneans conquered the island around 1450 BCE (Preziosi and Hitchcock 1999, 69). The find was a striking contrast to the generally peaceful frescoes discovered in the palace settlements, but indicative of the violent change that took place during the period. For the most part, the bronze weapons were similar to what were used by other peoples in the Mediterranean and Near East during the period, but an axe in particular piqued the interest of many scholars, some whom believed that it held the answer to the Phaistos Disc. The reason why some scholars believe that the "Arkalochori axe," as it is often known by, holds the key to the Phaistos Disc is because like the disk, it is incised with many of the same characters (Preziosi and Hitchcock 1999, 69). Unfortunately, also like the disk, the axe only contains the enigmatic characters and are not accompanied with a Linear B inscription that modern scholars could translate. The presence of some of the same characters on both the axe and the disk raises interesting questions concerning the purpose and context of the Phaistos Disc.

Most of the attempted translations of the Phaistos Disc discussed above – whether Linear A, Linear B, later Greek, Hittite, or Luwian – all supported the idea that the text was religious in nature. It is true that many, if not most texts from the Bronze Age were religious in nature, but the fact remains that it is still pure conjecture. Muenzer's argument that "business texts are never made so elaborately" (Muenzer 1985, 271) only may be true if the text is Greek, but if it was a variant of Linear A, which it seems more likely, then the argument may not hold water since Linear A is yet to be deciphered. By the end of the 20th century it appeared that all theories and potential translations of the Phaistos Disc had been exhausted; most new work was simply refutations and/or addendums to earlier published reports.

Recent Attempts to Decipher the Phaistos Disc

The 21st century would bring a new round of interesting if not necessarily solid attempts to translate the Phaistos Disc. By the early 2000s, interest in the Phaistos Disc had receded significantly among Aegean and classical scholars who have for the most part given up on deciphering its cryptic script. Classical and Aegean philologists have devoted most of their time to studying known Linear B texts and attempting to decipher the still enigmatic Linear A writing. To these scholars, for the most part, the Phaistos Disc is interesting, but its true significance will probably never be known because it will remain undeciphered. By the end of the decade, though, new scholarly interest in the Phaistos Disc came from outside the traditional Aegean and classical circles.

Recently, a Georgian scholar named Gia Kvashilava has published a number of articles, mainly in the Georgian language, about Linear A and its origins. Kvashilava believes that Linear A's origins can be found in his own country which in ancient times was known by the Greeks as Colchis. Kvashilava presented his findings, and a translation of the Phaistos Disc based on Colchian, at the International Conference of the Phaistos Disc on October 31, 2008 in London, England (Morritt 2010, 91). He believes that the disk's origins can be found in Georgia due to a fragment discovered in that country that has a Colchian inscription which bears a remarkable similarity to the signs on the Phaistos Disc. Kvashilava's translation was religious in nature and connected to agriculture and the growing season (Morritt 2010, 91). Although Kvashilava's translation has not caught much with academics around the world, it is considered a legitimate attempt to unravel the enigma of the Phaistos Disc. Another translation given at the 2008 conference is also worth mentioning.

Like Kvashilava, Andis Kaulins is a legitimate scholar who has dedicated much of his professional life to deciphering and understanding the Phaistos Disc. Also similar to Kvashilava, Kaulins has proposed an interesting decipherment of the disk that places its linguistic origins far from the Linear A homeland of Crete. At the 2008 conference, Kaulins proposed that he had discovered Elamite texts with symbols that were similar to those on the Phaistos Disc (Morritt 2010, 94). Kaulins then offered an Elamite translation that was religious in nature. Although Kaulins' theory and translation were arrived at on solid academic grounds, it does not make it correct and most Aegean scholars have not given the translation much attention. The same is true for most ancient Near Eastern scholars.

There are some major problems with Kaulins' theories that were simply overlooked by the scholar. Elamite was the language spoken by the Elamite people who lived in what is now western Iran until the late first millennium BCE. Scholars have so far been unable to place Elamite into any of the larger linguistic families – Semitic and Indo-European – which were used by peoples of the Near East at the time (Kuhrt 2010, 367). Although written Elamite employed the cuneiform script, much like the other contemporary languages of the Near East, the now published texts are limited in number and not completely understood. The lack of understanding of the Elamite language perhaps makes it an attractive assignment for the Phaistos Disc; since it is not completely understood, one can argue that the seemingly non-Elamite inscriptions on the disk are just a variant of the language. Most of the extant Elamite texts come from the period between 1300 and 1100 BCE (Kuhrt 2010, 367) which is long after the Phaistos Disc is believed to have been created. Although Elamite language documents are known from the period of the Phaistos Disc, they have all been discovered in Persia or Mesopotamia (Kuhrt 2010, 367). There are no known Elamite texts from Crete. This is not to say that Elamite text could not have ended up in Crete through trade, but it is an academic leap and an assumption to believe that the inscriptions on the Phaistos Disc are variants of Elamite.

The Phaistos Disc Today

Currently, the decipherment of the Phaistos Disc is of little interest to most academics in Aegean studies. There is an impasse that seems almost impossible to overcome so focus has been given not so much on its content, but more so its structure. Many scholars such as Duhoux (2000, 597) believe that the script is primarily phonetic in nature, but they also state that a more complete understanding of Linear A is required before any translation should even be attempted. In another recent article, Arie Cate proposed that part of the problem lies with the fact that all attempts to translate the disk have been based on a false assumption concerning how it is read. Most attempts to translate the Phaistos Disc have assumed that the two sides of the disk are to be read separately, one after the other. Cate has proposed that the disk is actually not one-dimensional in this sense, but rather two-dimensional – both sides are supposed to be read together (Cate 2011, 123). This is in interesting theory and possibly one that could help understand the content, but obviously, it does little to help if the meaning of the signs remains a mystery. As many scholars have recently all but given up on translating the disk, some have stated the obvious.

Whittaker (2005), among others, has recently argued that modern academics have essentially given the Phaistos Disc too much credit. Pointing to the obvious that the inscriptions on the Phaistos Disc do not match any known language, Whittaker argues that they do not represent any language at all, but instead are fake writing made by an illiterate person. She further argued that if anything, the disk resembles an ancient Egyptian game board. Whittaker's theory appears to be gaining momentum in academia, as nearly all avenues of translation appear to have been exhausted. In the words of Schwartz, who perhaps offered the most scholarly analysis of the disk, "Without further texts including possibly a bilingual, the hope of reading this text completely is remote." (Schwartz 1959. 105).

The Antikythera Mechanism

Discovery of the Mechanism

A few days before Easter 1900, a chance encounter on the floor of the Ionian Sea set in motion one of the most enduring and enigmatic chapters of classical archaeology.[1] A group of Greek sponge divers happened upon the ancient wreck of a Roman trading vessel dating to the second quarter of the first century BCE, bringing to the surface a staggering haul of artistic artifacts, hidden amongst which were the remains of a geared mechanism that shook the academic world to its very foundations. The device, since named the Antikythera mechanism, revealed a level of technical accomplishment and astronomical understanding thought not to have been possible for another millennium at least.

The tale of the discovery of the Antikythera wreck has since entered the lore of maritime archaeology. Returning from Tunisian waters, the sponge divers took refuge from a storm in the lee of a barren and almost uninhabited islet in the Ionian group known as Antikythera. Having

---

[1] Note: Some accounts erroneously list the date as 1901

dropped anchor, they decided to take advantage of the opportunity to explore a submerged rock shelf in the hope of finding sponges. A diver was sent down to a depth of about 140 feet, or 42 meters, where, to his utter astonishment, he discovered a substantial wreck site strewn with artifacts, including bronze and marble statues and hundreds of intact amphorae.

News of this discovery was communicated to the authorities in Athens, and within months, a salvage operation was underway. The initial finds were comprised of a spectacular consignment of art, including, alongside much else, the iconic *Antikythera Ephebe,* an enigmatic and exquisite portrayal in bronze of a naked youth dated to 340 BCE. However, within a horde of generally anonymous detritus brought up alongside pieces of more obvious interest, there was an unidentified lump of corroded bronze and wood that for the time being went unnoticed.[2]

---

[2] Note: It is perhaps also worth noting that limitations in diving and salvage technology limited the scope of the original expedition, which lasted until September 1903. But an exploratory expedition mounted in 1953 by Frédéric Dumas and Jacques Cousteau concluded that there remained a great deal more on the site to be discovered. However, further expeditions, one in 1976, once again led by Jacques Cousteau, and others in 2012 and 2014, went on to reveal that in fact very little of exceptional interest remained.

The Antikythera Ephebe

The small museum staff had found itself so overwhelmed by the work of examining, interpreting and cataloguing this spectacular haul that many crates of formless marble and verdigrised bronze were simply put to one side and left for later examination. Not until May 17, 1902, fully two years after the initial discovery, did Greek archaeologist and director of the museum Valerios Staïs happen to notice a series of faint inscriptions on one particular piece of rubble, finally realizing the significance of arguably the most important artifact to be recovered from the Antikythera wreck.

Staïs

Once the value of this strange object had been fully appreciated and an effort to preserve it begun, a considerable amount of criticism was leveled. How was it possible that an uneducated Greek sponge diver had been able to recognize the value of an object 40 meters below the surface of the Ionian Sea that the educated eyes of a team of trained archaeologists and researchers ignored for two years? It was also noted that over several months of the salvage, numerous delicate objects had been brought to the surface without significant breakage, only for this delicate mechanism to be left to dry out in the sun and split open when entrusted to the care of the academic staff of the museum.[3]

These were no doubt valid points, but it was precisely because the object had split open that Valerios Staïs had been able to peer into its heart and observe for the first time the tiny inscriptions engraved into its surface. Then, as he examined the object more closely, Staïs noticed the remnants of some internal mechanism hidden by lime and verdigrised bronze, and although he had no idea at the time what it was, he recognized its significance immediately.

Careful efforts at cleaning and preserving the object began in the hope of arresting any further damage, followed by an initial mapping and cataloguing of its fundamentals. While there was no obvious indication of what this object might be, or what its function was, what was apparent was that it was a device comprising relatively sophisticated gearing, superficially resembling clockwork.

---

[3] The Mechanism consisted of a series of bronze plates held together in a wooden frame or case, which was not preserved upon its retrieval, causing it to crack when exposed to dry air.

Pictures of salvaged fragments of the device

What is the Antikythera Mechanism?

The immediate effect of the discovery of this mechanism was to throw the original speculative dating of the wreck into doubt. It seemed impossible that a technical device of such finesse, delicacy and mastery could belong to the same era of antiquity as the other significant finds of the wreck. It was presumed, therefore, that either the wreck was a great deal more recent than imagined or that the device must have originated from a second and much later shipwreck.

Before the object could be dated, however, it had to be identified, which immediately set in motion a bitter academic squabble that would endure until World War II and the Axis occupation of Greece. The saga began against the backdrop of a science that was still very much in its infancy.

The Antikythera wreck had been one of the first important finds of its type to be recorded in the Mediterranean, and certainly one of the first significant exercises in marine archeology as a branch of science, so early Greek researchers examining the apparatus were at best groping their way through the dim light of an academic dawn. The first to attempt to do so, however, was Valerios Staïs himself, and what he had to work with was very little indeed.

Although tentatively cleaned, the mechanism consisted of little more than a small collection of indeterminate objects encrusted with limestone over most of their outer surfaces. Where the principal fragments had cracked, a blue/green of copper chloride blended with the red of copper oxide, and with various shades of tin oxide mingling to reveal just the faint and enigmatic traces of a tangled mechanism within. The largest fragment, measuring about six by five inches, held a large four-spoked wheel, almost the size of the fragment itself, into the diameter of which had been cut about 200 teeth. A second and smaller toothed wheel appeared to engage with the larger, while several additional cogwheels were visible on the back. Inscriptions were also visible, although not at that point decipherable.

A second, slightly smaller fragment appeared to have a flat sheet of bronze attached to it, upon which were also engraved a series of inscriptions. On the back of this had been cut a series of concentric circles, which seemed from initial observation to serve as guides for a rotating pointer.[4] In total, at least 15 interlocking gears were visible.

Staïs' initial impression was that the object had to have been some kind of perpetual motion clockwork mechanism. However, a span of a thousand years or more stood between even a liberal dating of this wreck and the emergence of the first mechanical clocks in medieval Europe. Staïs, therefore, modified this initial theory, concluding in the end that the device must have been some sort of measuring or calculating instrument.

Even this, however, challenged his credulity. Prior to this discovery, not a single gearwheel had been unearthed that could be attributable to Greek antiquity, and indeed, that remains the case today. It is true that ancient classical texts hint at the existence, or at least the knowledge of gearing, as early as the 3rd century BCE, but these, like the Archimedes Screw, tended to be simple devices involving the crude engagement of two or three gears at the most, typically to apply force or lift a weight.[5] Nothing of this complexity was thought to have been possible until the development of clockwork many centuries later.

Realizing that he probably lacked the expertise to accurately interpret the mechanism, Staïs introduced two new experts into the field; the first was a brilliant but eccentric Greek numismatist by the name of John Svoronos, and the second a no less brilliant young Austrian inscriptionist by the name of Adolf Wilhelm. On May 23, 1902, a report in the Greek newspaper *To Asty* stated that Staïs, with the help of these two men, had identified the object as some sort of an *Astrolabe*.[6] Further reports added that Wilhelm had partially read the visible inscriptions, and

---

[4] Marchant, Jo (2009-02-10). *Decoding the Heavens: A 2,000-Year-Old Computer--and the Century-long Search to Discover Its Secrets* (p. 39). Da Capo Press. Kindle Edition.

[5] Two such devices were the *Baroulkos* and the *Dioptra*, the former a simple lifting device and the latter an astronomical and surveying instrument.

[6] An *astrolabe* (Greek: *astrolabos, star-taker*) is an elaborate inclinometer, historically used by astronomers, navigators, and astrologers. Among its uses was the location and prediction of the positions of the Sun, Moon, planets, and stars, establishing time according to local coordinates, and vice versa, surveying, and triangulation. It was used in classical antiquity, the Islamic Golden Age, the European Middle Ages and Renaissance for all these purposes. In the Islamic world, it was also used to calculate the Qibla and to find the times for prayers –

had thus dated the mechanism to between the 2nd century BCE and the 2nd century AD.

Then, Greek naval historian, and later curator of the National Historical Museum in Athens, Professor Konstantinos *Rados, weighed in, and clouded the waters even further, by claiming, upon careful examination of the fragments, that the device could not have been an astrolabe, at least not according to any contemporary understanding of such a device. He instead asserted that the mechanism was a spring driven clockwork apparatus, proving in his mind at least that it must have originated from a second, much later wreck on the same site.*

It was John Svoronos, however, in collaboration with a certain Pericles Rediadis, eminent Greek professor of geodesy and hydrography, who authored the first written report on the mechanism. Rediadis felt confident that he had identified from among the various inscriptions, the Greek word μοιρογνωμονιον. This, according to modern interpretation, translates to protractor, but which, in ancient Greek, tended more to imply a reference to the zodiac scale. It was a word that could also be identified amongst the earliest known descriptions of an astrolabe mechanism attributed to the Coptic scientist and philosopher John Philoponus (490 –570 AD) of Alexandria, reproduced in his treatise *On the Use and Construction of the Astrolabe,* published in the mid-6th century.

With this, the ball was returned. *Clearly, this "completely strange instrument," which resembled nautical instruments contained in wooden boxes that were still typical at the turn of the nineteenth century, was related in some way to astronomy, and so, in the opinion of the Svoronos and Rediadis, it must indeed have been an astrolabe.*

The authors of the report did concede, however, that if the instrument was an astrolabe, then it was certainly unlike any astrolabe ever discovered before, or ever recorded in historic texts. This prompted Svoronos to venture a more conservative date of the third century AD for the mechanism, although privately he was apt to speculate that it was much later than even that.

In the meanwhile, in 1905, Konstantinos Rados published his own paper, which disputed Svoronos' theory, arguing instead that the mechanism was far too complicated to be an astrolabe. He insisted that the device comprised a spring driven mechanism that functioned in perpetual motion, which, under the circumstances, was a logical position backed up a few years later by a young German inscriptionist by the name of Albert Rehm.

Rehm studied Rados' report, but frustrated by its lack of detail, travelled to Athens himself in order to study the device at first hand. Upon a cursory examination, he felt comfortable concurring with Rados that the device was indeed far too complicated to be an astrolabe.

In the meanwhile, as this ebb and flow of academic debate continued, the fragments underwent cleaning and preservation, which, although controversial, nonetheless did at least clarify previously identified markings and reveal new ones. Consequently, Albert Rehm was able to identify what he recognised as the word ΠΑΧΩΝ (on the main front dial of the instrument on Fragment C), or Pachon.

Pachon, Pashons or Bashans, is variously the ninth month of the Coptic calendar, the first month of the harvest season in the Egyptian calendar, April in the Julian calendar and May in the

Gregorian calendar. From this Rehm concluded two things. Firstly, there would be no practical need for months to be inscribed on a conventional astrolabe, and secondly that the mechanism must have succeeded the Roman calendar reform of 46 BCE that introduced the Julian Calendar.

While this interpretation of the inscription might well have been correct, it was immediately disputed that this in fact implied a date post the Julian calendar, since reference to the Egyptian style of the word *ΠΑΧΩΝ* had been noted in historic texts as early as the works of Plato and Ptolemy. Rehm's suggestion also that the object might in some way relate to a planetarium device, similar to the *Sphere of Archimedes*, was also fairly early shot down, since the device was obviously not configured in a sphere, and nor was there any evidence of it having any hydraulic mechanism.

Thereafter, notwithstanding periodic renewals of the squabble, the debate ebbed, punctuated periodically by studies and reports, most notably that of John Theophanides. Theophanides was a rear admiral in the Greek navy who became interested in the mechanism during the 1920s as he researched a biographical account of the maritime journeys of St. Paul. In a 1934 report, he noted a graded scale around the circumference of a large ring revealed under cleaning on the front fascia, and further, that the main, cross-shaped gear wheel drove the rotation of several smaller wheels, describing a crank at the side that appeared to be driven by the main wheel. All of this suggested a clockwork device wound by hand, or perhaps driven by a water clock.

His conclusion, however, did little to advance matters. While not entirely disowning the astrolabe theory, the mechanism, Theophanides suggested, was in fact a navigational device with the various descriptions being personal to the captain to whom it belonged. Perhaps it was intended to calculate the precise positions of the sun, moon and planets, with the gearing ratios replicating their relative movements. He also speculated that by setting various pointers on the device according to the shadow cast by a nail placed in the middle of the concentric circles, it could calculate, by means of the gearing, the precise orientation of the ship. All of this, of course, was wildly speculative, proving in the end that no one had clue what the device was or how old it was.

A New Age

With the rise of fascism in Europe and the eventual occupation of Greece, the question of the Antikythera mechanism followed the device itself into protective storage. Most of the principal antiquities in the Athens Museum of Archeology were hidden away to avoid looting, and for the duration of the war, and for some time afterwards, the mechanism remained hidden under the floorboards of the museum. It would not be until the early 1950s that a new generation of scientific interest would take root.

The sum total of what had been achieved thus far had been rather limited. A few scattered historic references, the name *Pachon* and a zodiac scale all tended to suggest that the purpose of the device was astronomical rather than navigational, and perhaps that it had been part of the ship's cargo rather that an instrument of navigation, but besides this there was very little that could be definitively stated. It was Greek and it was dated somewhere between the second century BCE and the third century AD, and that was all.

Attention then shifted to the cargo of the ship, with academics, including Staïs and Svoronos, tending to look more closely at the art and artifacts associated with the wreck as a means of dating it and determining its port of origin. This, however, would prove no less imprecise, since any artifact might have been in existence for centuries before being purchased, stolen or looted. More profitable might be an examination of the more mundane artifacts collected in the salvage, such as pottery and amphora, which would have been in daily use and thus more likely to reflect the precise period of manufacture.

Two women, American archaeologist Virginia Grace and her Greek associate Maria Savvatianou, took up the baton. In 1954, as both women were working on the relatively routine project of cataloguing thousands of broken and partial amphorae unearthed across the Mediterranean, Savvatianou happened to come across John Svoronos' 1903 paper in which the general catalogue from the Antikythera wreck had been described, including a monochrome photograph of the various amphora. Maria Savvatianou suggested that if those amphorae could be located and dated, it might then be possible to affix a more accurate date to the wreck.

By then, a half-century after the discovery of the Antikythera wreck, hundreds of similar sites had been located and studied across the Mediterranean, with a great deal of work undertaken there, as well as on various land sites, in classifying and understanding such day-to-day items as amphorae. A detailed comparison of materials and styles could very possibly identify, not only the likely date of the wreck, but also its port of origin. Thus, a small team of interested parties and experts assembled to undertake this work, among them Henry Robinson, Director of the American School of Classical Studies at Athens (ASCSA), Roger Evans from the University of Pennsylvania, Gladys Weinberg of the University of Missouri and journalist and maverick archaeologist Peter Throckmorton.

This enigmatic team of scientists, historians and archaeologists mobilized and set to work, and despite significant practical difficulties, and no small amount of squabbling and professional rivalry, the results that they achieved were impressive. Throckmorton, after considerable research and analysis, determined that the wood used in the construction of the wreck had been elm originating from central Italy, confirming the ships Roman origins. Then, using groundbreaking technology for the time, fragments of the superstructure were carbon dated to between 260 and 180 BCE.[7]

Conceivably, however, the ship could have been in service for decades before it sunk, which left a wide margin of error. Nonetheless, this general parameter conformed more to Staïs' theory that the ship had sunk in the 2nd century BCE than that of Svoronos' estimation of 300 CE. However, these new discoveries also served simply to deepen the general enigma, for quite clearly, if the Antikythera mechanism had gone down with the ship, then even with a century of error either way, classical Mediterranean societies must have been in possession of technologies far in advance of anything hitherto attributed.

For the time being, however, the mystery of the mechanism itself remained of secondary

[7] Marchant, Jo (2009-02-10). Decoding the Heavens: A 2,000-Year-Old Computer--and the Century-long Search to Discover Its Secrets (p. 73). Da Capo Press. Kindle Edition.

interest to the study of the ship and its general cargo. From the amphorae, it was further established that the ship had started its journey from somewhere along the coast of Asia Minor between about 86 and 60 BCE. It was laden with cargo probably looted by a Roman occupying force, and en-route to the home of a prominent general, perhaps even Lucius Cornelius Sulla, or Pompey himself.

The exact location of this port was narrowed down further by a small haul of coinage brought up from the wreck by divers associated with the Cousteau/Dumas expedition of 1976. These where, of course, marked and dated, and ultimately proved to be silver coins from the ancient Greek city of Pergamon, located on the modern day coast of Turkey. Most were speculatively dated between 85-76 BCE, which suggested that the ship sank sometime between 70 and 60 BCE.

This was not to say that the date of the original manufacture of the Antikythera mechanism was precisely during this period. If, however, it could be identified as a ship's instrument, and part of the on-board equipment, then in all likelihood it would not predate the ship itself by very much. On the other hand, if proved more arcane than simply a navigational device, and part of the ship's cargo, then it might conceivably be more ancient still.

Therefore, quite obviously, until the exact nature of the machine itself could be decoded, it would remain no more than an enigma, an archaeological curiosity. Dating coins and amphorae associated with the wreck could only achieve so much. The wreck itself had more or less been dated, identified and catalogued, but the Antikythera mechanism remained a mystery. The baton was then passed into the hands of a British physicist, historian and scientist by the name of Derek John de Solla Price.

Understanding the Mechanism

Derek Price and the Antikythera Model

Derek Price's Wikipedia page opens with this rather bland assessment of a most extraordinary scientific and academic career: "Derek John de Solla Price (22 January 1922 – 3 September 1983) was a physicist, historian of science, and information scientist, credited as the father of scientometrics." Perhaps more revealing is an attached photograph of Price as an older man, his lavish, trademark briar-wood pipe in hand, and appearing somewhat self-satisfied as he displays an expanded reconstruction of the Antikythera mechanism on a table before him. That sense of self-satisfaction also hints a little at the professional arrogance that Price was so often accused of, and of which he was certainly guilty. However, without that very self-possession, it is unlikely that he would have advanced his research in the mechanism to the extent that he did, and nor would he have produced the first working model that began the three dimensional understanding of something that almost defied understanding.

Born in 1922, Derek Price was a member of a gifted generation, endowed with the attributes of British imperial hubris at a time when the English speaking races predominated, and when English speaking intellectuals and academics permeated and conquered almost every discipline of formal study. It is also true that on a personal level he was gifted with undeniable brilliance, extraordinary drive and an insatiable curiosity, all of which, in combination with a conundrum that he could really sink his teeth into, ensured a career with all of those thoroughly British attributes of eccentricity and genius.

The legend that has formed around Derek Price begins with his first childhood encounter with a construction set, a Meccano set in fact, which triggered a lifelong fascination with mechanics and mechanical devices.[8] Born in the East End of London to humble parentage, he was, along

---

[8] *Meccano* is a model construction system created in Liverpool by British toy maker Frank Hornby, and which consists of reusable metal strips,

with a generation of boys, transported by science fiction pamphlets and comic books inspired by the genesis of advanced technology. In 1942, he earned his first degree in physics and mathematics from the University of London, after which, thanks to critical personnel shortages occasioned by WWII, he was absorbed by the university as a lecturer. In 1946, he earned his first PhD for his original research on behalf of the military into the optical qualities of molten metal.

After the War he took up a teaching position at the Raffles College of Singapore, precursor to the current National University of Singapore, were he pioneered the study of scientometrics, the measuring and study of science itself. His passion for instrumentation, however, began to gather pace when he left Singapore and enrolled in Cambridge University to pursue a second PhD. His thesis on this occasion focused on the history of modern scientific instruments.

His interest in ancient instrumentation, however, began when he read Geoffrey Chaucer's late fourteenth century publication, Treatise on the Astrolabe, one of the earliest works in English describing an elaborate scientific instrument. This prompted Price, now in his mid-thirties, to begin a specialization in the history of astronomical instruments, beginning with the simple sundial, and continuing through the evolution of the astrolabe and the equatorium.[9]

Part of his study involved an examination of early Chinese experiments in clocks and clockwork, and the influence this might have had on similar technologies in Europe. Advanced clockwork technology seemed to have appeared in Medieval Europe, apparently without any progenitor, thanks largely to the sudden manifestation of an escapement mechanism.[10] The escapement mechanism, an elegantly simple solution to perpetual motion, was one of the defining moments in the evolution of mechanical technology. With the addition of steam power, it led directly to industrialization and mass production, in particular in the development of the power loom and automated weaving.[11]

However, history has tended to credit European innovation with the invisible development of this early clockwork technology. Price, however, theorized that the early development of this technology began in China centuries earlier, and in the classical world earlier still, arriving in Europe more or less fully evolved sometime during the early Renaissance period. Clearly, Price reasoned, complicated gearing and leaps of technology like the escapement mechanism could hardly have happened overnight, as the historic record would tend to suggest, but rather were built on a technological evolution begun elsewhere, perhaps in China, but certainly somewhere else before that.

Then, in the midst of this train of thought, Price happened upon the various papers written by

---

plates, angle girders, wheels, axles and gears, with nuts and bolts to connect the pieces. It enables the building of working models and mechanical devices.

[9] An *equatorium* is an astronomical calculating instrument used for locating the relative positions of the Moon, Sun, and planets without calculation, using a geometrical model to represent the position of a given celestial body.

[10] An *Escapement* is a mechanism in a clock or watch that alternately checks and releases the train by a fixed amount and transmits a periodic impulse from the spring or weight to the balance wheel or pendulum.

[11] Note: *An escapement* is a key element in mechanical watches and clocks that transfers energy to the timekeeping element, the *impulse action*, which allows the number of its oscillations to be counted and regulated in a *locking action*. The impulse action transfers energy to the clock's timekeeping element, typically a pendulum or balance wheel, but also a winding-spring, to replace energy lost to friction during its cycle, and to keep the timekeeper oscillating.

Svoronos, Rados and Rehm, at which point his theory seemed more or less confirmed. Moreover, it amazed him that the Antikythera mechanism could have been ignored by the mechanical sciences for so long, when quite evidently this little mechanism represented a vital link in a fractured technological lineage that clearly had its roots somewhere deep in darkest antiquity.

In 1953, therefore, he wrote to the then curator of the National Archaeological Museum in Athens, a certain Christos Karouzos, requesting any new information that might be available on the mechanism. What he learned was that, although there had been no further study of the device since the 1920s, cleaning and examination had revealed a considerable amount of hitherto unstudied detail. Again, it struck Price as almost unbelievable that the academic world had for so long ignored this obviously critical archaeological find. In an article published in the British scientific journal Discovery, he commented that, if genuine, the Antikythera mechanism must surely require a complete re-evaluation of ancient Greek technology, adding that its discovery must at the time have been akin to opening the tomb of Tutankhamen to discover the decayed but recognizable parts of an internal combustion engine.[12]

In 1958, he travelled to Athens for a first-hand look at the mechanism, and came face to face with "a forgotten strand of invention whose threads he sees woven into everything around him, in every car and bicycle, every clock and calculator."[13] However, even though his view of the device was arguably more definitive than any who had come before him, he was no less perplexed and intrigued by its facets.

The first fact that he was able to confirm, however, with the help of an eminent Greek epigrapher by the name of George Stamires, was that the various legible inscriptions, now enhanced to some 800 individual characters, did indeed date to the first century BCE, which, of course, correlated with earlier dating suggested by Virginia Grace et al. It was also apparent to Price that the fragments were not disparate parts of a larger device, but a complete mechanism, or at least most of it. It was also apparent to him that the pieces all fitted together and interacted with one another for the purpose of calculation. What precisely that calculation sought to achieve, however, remained, for the time being at least, a mystery. It also seemed likely that the mechanism had not been crushed or compressed, as previously thought, but had been constructed on various flat planes, which allowed at least for some educated speculation on its function.

Price reckoned that at least 20 gearwheels had survived in fragments, with each apparently cut from a flat sheet of bronze about two millimeters thick. In the centre of the mechanism was a flat bronze plate with an arrangement of gearwheels above and below, and driven by an axle entering through the side of the case, which in turn drove a small crown wheel positioned parallel to the side of the box, and at right angles to the rest of the gearwheels. The crown wheel then engaged with the larger, four-spoked wheel to drive all of the other gears.

Like his predecessors, Price believed that the mechanism had originally been contained in a rectangular wooden box resembling an eighteenth century coach clock. Much of what he then

---

[12] *Discovery*, April 1957 Edition.

[13] Marchant, Jo (2009-02-10). Decoding the Heavens: A 2,000-Year-Old Computer--and the Century-long Search to Discover Its Secrets (p. 109). Da Capo Press. Kindle Edition.

concluded from careful examination was speculative, although substantively accurate. On the front of the case was located a large central dial, probably with a handle, and almost as wide as the case itself, while on the back there were two smaller dials of the same width, one above the other. There also appeared to be small doors on the front and back made of flat bronze plates. Engraved upon these bronze surfaces, as well as the front and back faces, were various inscriptions.

Turning his attention to the front dial, only the bottom portion of which had survived, Price noted two scales around its edge. However, by counting the gradations he was able to estimate that the inner scale was divided into 12 sections of 30, totaling 360.

In the meanwhile, on the bottom segment of the same (front) dial, George Stamires was able to decipher the complete word XHΛAI, or Chelai in ancient Greek, meaning claws, which implied the claws of Scorpio. Counter-clockwise on the dial it was possible to discern just two letters – NO – which was enough to suggest the name of the preceding zodiac sign of Virgo, or Parthenos in Greek.

The mechanism's scale, therefore, strongly suggested 360 degrees of the Greek zodiac, with twelve signs running clockwise around its edge, and with the additional likelihood that a pointer of some sort traced the dial in order to mark the Sun's annual movement, as perceived at the time. The outer ring, in the meanwhile, was divided into 365 segments, inscribed with the month name Pachon (ΠAXΩN), as initially identified by Rehm, and the first two letters of Payni (ΠA . . .), or two consecutive months of the ancient Greco-Egyptian calendar visible in the surviving top portion.

To the experienced eye of a man like Price, what he was obviously looking at was a scale showing the months of the year running clockwise around the dial, with a pointer on the inner dial plotting the sun's path against a backdrop of stars, while the outer scale would speculatively have indicated the date. This appeared to conform to a calendar system known and utilized throughout the Hellenistic world, popular simply because each year had precisely the same sequence of months and days. The only drawback to this was that it did not account for the modern leap year adjustment. Consequently, Price concluded, massaging the evidence somewhat to suit his theory, the outer ring must be rotatable in order to be able to compensate.

Additional inscriptions etched into the scale, and which were only partially decipherable, appeared to refer to such astronomical events as "Vega rises in the evening", "The Hyades set in the morning" and "Gemini begins to rise."[14] These inscriptions were immediately familiar to Price from the various parapegma that he had studied in the past, their typical purpose being to relate these repeating astronomical events with annual phenomena taking place on Earth, such as seasonal shifts, rainfall patterns and the flooding of the Nile. [15] Obviously, the inscriptions on the Antikythera mechanism had been intended to serve a similar purpose.

---

[14] Marchant, Jo (2009-02-10). Decoding the Heavens: A 2,000-Year-Old Computer--and the Century-long Search to Discover Its Secrets (p. 112). Da Capo Press. Kindle Edition.

[15] *Parapegma* – an antecedent of the modern day almanac. Originally a table relating star phases to corresponding weather predictions. Early versions were carved on stone, and had holes next to the descriptions, marking each day. The peg could be advanced each day, and on appropriate days the associated inscription would "predict" certain astronomical and meteorological events.

On the back of the mechanism, in the meanwhile, were two dials, one above the other, the function of which Price could only guess. Each seemed to comprise a series of concentric rings, perhaps five above and four below, divided into segments of about six degrees each. Upon these segments were inscribed strings of letters and numbers whose meaning was unclear, and on each back dial there was offset a miniature dial. The inscriptions on the back of the device seemed less coherent than those on the front, with the few legible words suggesting that these were some sort of operating instruction peculiar to the original owner or user.

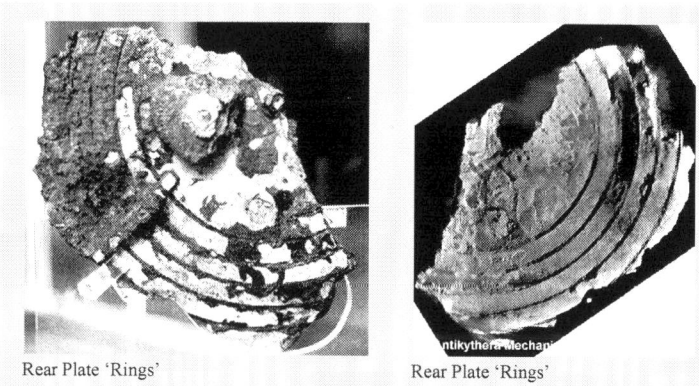

Rear Plate 'Rings'   Rear Plate 'Rings'

All of this, while at the very least fascinating, and to some degree illuminating, did not ultimately shed any light on the actual function of the device. However, the Antikythera mechanism, although not necessarily showing hours and minutes, was nonetheless, in Price's opinion, concerned with "time, in its most fundamental sense, measured by the wheeling of celestial bodies through the heavens."[16]

And there, for the time being, matters rested. Returned to its cigar box, the mechanism was reburied in the vaults of the Archaeological Museum of Athens while Price returned to his academic career. Soon afterwards, he took a job at the prestigious Institute for Advanced Study at Princeton University where he lectured on mathematics and scientometrics, but also at every opportunity on the subject of the Antikythera mechanism.[17]

---

[16] Marchant, Jo (2009-02-10). Decoding the Heavens: A 2,000-Year-Old Computer--and the Century-long Search to Discover Its Secrets (p. 115). Da Capo Press. Kindle Edition.

[17] Note: Price's work on the Antikythera Mechanism attracted the attention of Science Fiction Writer Arthur C. Clarke who became a powerful advocate and supporter of Price's work and research. During a lecture to the Smithsonian Institution in Washington DC., soon after the first lunar landing, Clarke commented that had the Greeks had been able to build on their knowledge, the Industrial Revolution might have begun more than a millennium earlier. *"By this time we would not merely be pottering around on the Moon. We would have reached the nearer stars."*

From Princeton Price moved to Yale, and there continued to ponder his notes and drawings, slowly beginning to form a more coherent picture of the mechanism and its likely assembly and function. Returning to Athens in 1962, he again sat for many hours carefully examining the device, taking notes and conceptualizing the relationship of the surviving gears. In the meanwhile, on behalf of National Geographic, he studied the Tower of the Winds in Athens, which gave him the opportunity to indulge a little more in his obsession with the Antikythera mechanism. He studied it when he could, eventually reaching the conclusion that, until a working replica of the mechanism could be created, the genius of its construction would always remain elusive.

Sadly, however, there was not enough data available to speculate on any accurate assembly of gears, and until technology could provide the means to look deeper into the heart of the surviving pieces, its inner functions would remain a mystery. Sometime later, however, Price happened to glance through a technical report published by researchers at Oak Ridge National Laboratory in Tennessee, describing how gamma rays from radioactive isotopes could be used to peer inside metallic objects of archaeological importance without destroying them. This was precisely what he had been waiting for. He wrote immediately to the director of Oak Ridge asking if this new imaging technique could be used to study the Antikythera Mechanism.

Reconsidering Ancient Greek Technology

Through Oakridge, Price was introduced to the Greek Atomic Energy Commission and a nuclear physicist by the name of Charalambos Karakalos. Karakalos was head of radiology at a nuclear research laboratory in Athens, and although initially skeptical, he was in the end persuaded to subject the main fragments of the mechanism to X-ray exposure. The initial results proved to be encouraging enough for him to delve further, and over the course of the summer of 1972, his experimentations produced hundreds of new images, achieving nothing less than a revolutionary new insight into the inner workings of the mechanism.

Price returned to Athens soon afterwards to study these new images, and for the first time was able to make a relatively accurate appraisal of how the various wheels had been arranged, which ones meshed with which and the numbers of teeth on each. Armed with this information, and the plethora of new images, he returned to Yale, and there set about trying to map the blueprint of a replica.

The difficulty, of course, lay in the fact that the ghosted images on radiographic paper tended to superimpose the gears with no clear indication of their order of assembly. In a process of trial and error, he used a series of cardboard replicas and speculative manipulation of numbers and layers to try to determine precisely how the main wheel was driven, how it interacted with the assembly and for what ultimate purpose.

The original tooth counts on the gears, which had been calculated and recorded by Charalambos Karakalos' wife, could be assumed to be substantively accurate, at least within a tooth or two. Price, however, took considerable liberty with the results, and from this, and according to the placements of the gears indicated on the radiographic images, he was able to establish a sequence of gearing ratios related broadly to a contemporary perception of solar and lunar movements in relation to one another.

From this emerged the first three dimensional replica of the device, which, bearing in mind the limitations that he had worked under, was an achievement indeed. Price, however, was perhaps guilty of too much speculation, and no small amount of manipulation of evidence to suit his theory. He embarked on his investigation with the presupposition that the mechanism was some sort of a "computer" used to calculate astronomical events in the near or distant future – the next full moon as the most likely example. Clearly, the inscriptions on the large dial were calendrical, indicating months and days along with signs of the zodiac. He theorized – accurately as it would transpire – that there must have been pointers and arms, now missing, that represented the sun, the moon and quite possibly the known planets, and that these pointers moved around the face of the dial indicating the position of the heavenly bodies at any given time.[18]

In his subsequent publication, Gears from the Greeks, it is clear, despite his narrative being extraordinarily difficult to follow, that Price did indeed make significant leaps of faith and jumps of logic that one can assume made perfect sense only in his mind. With the benefit of more advanced imaging technology, later researchers and academics have tended to heap scorn on this first great step, and only with the benefit of hindsight is there perhaps some justification for this.

Derek Price was without doubt an arrogant and self-possessed individual, a failing not uncommon among leading academics, and he was certainly far too quick to sign off on his efforts as the last definitive word necessary on the matter. He was, however, very much on the right track. The secret to decoding this mechanism lay in part in simple mathematics and mechanical ratios, but also perhaps with a more philosophical quotient. It required an instinctual understanding the subject, of astronomy and Greek history, but also it demanded a less definable ability to channel directions from his peers and equals who resided in the darkest antiquity.

Did he succeed? Not entirely, but it's important to at least consider his methods. He began with the basic assumption that the largest gear in the artifact, fragment A, was tied to the movements of the sun, with a single rotation equaling one solar year. If the movement of the moon was indicated through the turning of a second gear, driven by the solar gear, this must have been calculated to accord with the Greek idea of the moon's movements. By counting the number of teeth in each gear, it ought theoretically to be possible to calculate the gear ratios, and then, by comparing those ratios to astronomical cycles, it would be possible, again theoretically, to determine which gears represented which movements.[19]

So what came first: knowing the mathematics or understanding the fundamentals of ancient Greek astronomical theory? It is hard to say, but the net result of his computations was a calendar sequence related to the lunar cycle (as opposed to the solar cycle upon which the modern calendar is configured), the imprecision of which was compensated for by the return of the moon to precisely the same position relative to the sun every 19-years.

This is known as the Metonic cycle.[20] According to this cycle, the number of sidereal months

[18] Seabrook, John. Flash of Genius: And Other True Stories of Invention. (St. Martins, New York, 2008) p145
[19] Seabrook, John. Flash of Genius: And Other Stories of Invention. (St. Martins, New York, 2008) p145

[20] Metonic cycle defines a period of 19 years (235 lunar months), after which the new and full moons return to the same days of the year. It was the basis of the ancient Greek calendar and is still used for calculating movable feasts such as Easter.

in one year is 254/19.[21] Price, therefore, realized that, with a wheel that turns with the sun through the sky, it becomes possible to multiply its rotation by this ratio to calculate the speed of the moon. Manipulating the tooth counts by a unit here and there, Price was able to bring the ultimate resolution alluringly close to the 19-year cycle.

As satisfying as this was, it was nonetheless incomplete, since the conundrum that this theory presented was that each time a gearwheel meshed with another, the direction of rotation would be reversed. Consequently, the gear train that Price had just calculated would have spun the moon in reverse. Pondering this, he concluded that there must have been a second wheel of the same size as the wheel driving the sun pointer, now lost, and driven by the other side of the crown wheel, turning at the same speed, although in the opposite direction. To cope with the differentials in speed and timing of lunar and solar cycles, Price concluded that somewhere within the cluster of gearwheels there must have been a differential gear.

This notion, bold in the extreme, presupposed a gearing solution to a problem of relative motion so elegant in its conception that it simply could not have been the accidental discovery of one isolated genius. A differential gear could only have been the culmination of generations of trial, error and development, and this made the Antikythera Mechanism an even more astonishing phenomenon still.

It was, however, a characteristically long shot. After all, the first categorical record of a differential gearing system in use was that employed in 1720 by English clock maker Joseph Williamson. Anecdotal records do exist of differential systems being used in various devices in China as early as 2600 BCE, but the practical use of such a system in the Antikythera Mechanism would have predated any other known example by more than a millennium.

Assuming all of this to be true, however, the outstanding question remained simply what function the upper back dial served. Based on the visible evidence, this section of the device would seem to consist of a series of concentric rings, with a secondary dial divided into four, but with only part of the associated gear train surviving, it again became a matter of speculation. Price guessed that this wheel displayed the months of a four-year cycle that probably enabled the user to keep track of the 365-day calendar as it shifted against the seasons. What the specifics of this were, however, he could not guess.

He had, however, decoded the crucial elements of the apparatus, after which he felt confident enough to declare that the device was a "calendar computer," intended to calculate the movements of the Sun and Moon as seen from Earth, in order to track the days and months of the year, and to predict the corresponding position of the stars.[22]

The result of this marathon inquiry was Price's seminal paper, Gears from the Greeks, published in June 1974 to some academic acclaim, but also to no small amount of skepticism. The device, in the opinion of one eminent American academic at least, was simply a planetarium, of the sort that schoolchildren used to study the basics of planetary alignment, something that

---

[21] *Sidereal Month* defines the time it takes the moon to orbit once around the earth with respect to the stars (approximately 27 1/4 days)

[22] Marchant, Jo (2009-02-10). Decoding the Heavens: A 2,000-Year-Old Computer--and the Century-long Search to Discover Its Secrets (p. 149). Da Capo Press. Kindle Edition.

must have fallen on the site of the wreck centuries after it sank. Derek Price, he declared, was deluded.

In fairness, the principal assertion in Price's account – the use in the mechanism of a differential gear – could hardly have been construed as anything other than outlandish, and this he was prepared to admit.

"In my experience." He wrote, "It is difficult even today [to explain] the theory of this gear-work to the bulk of people in a modern audience familiar with a host of mechanical and electronic devices. It must surely rank as one of the greatest basic mechanical inventions of all time, and whether the inventor was Archimedes himself or some unknown genius mechanic of the school of Posidonios, he should be accorded the highest honors"[23]

Price's argument supporting his theory, although thin on facts, was nonetheless persuasive under the essential assertion that such a complicated mechanical concept as a differential gear could hardly have arrived in use in late sixteenth century clockwork without some sort of lineage. The mechanism, he wrote, "requires us to completely rethink our attitudes to ancient Greek technology."[24] The mechanism could also not have been one of a kind. No technology so sophisticated could simply appear suddenly, and fully realized.

Not so, argued another writer and theorist of the same era, a certain Erich von Däniken. Von Däniken, the Swiss author of the controversial 1968 publication Chariots of the Gods?, argued that it was aliens from the nether reaches of space who had seeded the earth with such advanced technology, facilitating also such marvels as the Egyptian pyramids, Stonehenge, the Moai of Easter Island and of course the Antikythera mechanism. This dispensed with the need for evolution or antecedent, adding the phenomenon of the Antikythera mechanism to a long list of crank mysteries, and tending to relegate Price to the pseudoscientific fringe.

Chariots of the Gods?, in the meanwhile, went on to sell millions, while Gears from the Greeks disappeared in a puff of scorn and academic skepticism. However, whatever its merits or deficiencies, Gears from the Greeks would prove to be Price's last word on the matter. Although disappointed with its reception, Price nonetheless felt that what could be understood and written about in reference to the Antikythera mechanism was contained in his thesis, and that neither he nor anyone else need go any further. He then began to apply his mind to the next great leap of future technology, electronic computerization, sadly dying of a heart attack in 1983, and right on the cusp of this era of new technology.

---

[23] De Solla Price, Derek. *Gears from the Greeks: The Antikythera Mechanism – a Calendar Computer from ca. 80 B.C. Transactions of the American Philosophical Society*, Volume 64. Part 7, 1974, p60.

[24] Thompson, Clive. *The Best of technology Writing 2008*. (University of Michigan Press, Ann Arbor, 2008) p78

Replication and Reconstruction

A 2007 reproduction of the mechanism

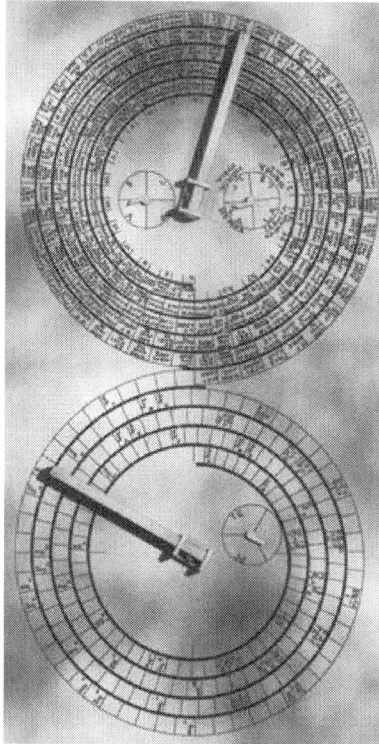
Picture of a computer generated back panel

One of the many skeptics unsold on the conclusions of Gears from the Greeks was Michael T. Wright, curator of mechanical engineering at the Science Museum of London, and the next to take up the baton of the Antikythera mechanism. His chapter of the story began when tasked to examine an artifact presented for sale to the museum by a Lebanese national claiming to have purchased it a few weeks earlier at a Beirut street market. The device proved to be an elaborate geared sundial of Greek origin, which was eventually purchased by the Science Museum.

Wright's research into the origins of the device, however, required a considerable amount of detective work, part of which included a review of the Derek Prices' Gears from the Greeks, which caused Wright to bristle somewhat. Betraying just a little bit of professional spite, Wright later wrote:

"I was compelled to re-read Price's paper with care, and began to notice objections to his account. Price contradicted himself, and contradicted or ignored detail that could be seen in the illustrations; he appealed to arguments concerning the design and execution of mechanic's work that carried little or no conviction, or even made no sense at all; and his reconstruction was both bizarre and incomplete"[25]

Despite this extremely uncharitable tone, Wright was nonetheless correct in his general assessment. Price certainly had played fast and loose with the results of the original tooth counts, adapting them to suit his theories rather than the other way. For a gearwheel labeled E5, for example, Mrs. Karakalos had estimated 50-52 teeth, but Price settled on 48 as more "appropriate," and for wheel G2, Karakalos had counted 54 or 55 teeth, but Price had dismissed this as "too small for any simple or meaningful interpretation of the gear train," suggesting a figure of 60 instead.[26]

To Wright, who was an experienced clockmaker and historian, it was quite clear that Price had utilized practical arguments to justify manipulating the facts in a manner that seemed to make no sense at all. Clearly, a significant amount of Price's difficulty had lain in determining the spatial relationship between the closely compacted features seen in his early radiographic images. Thus, in an uneasy partnership with Australian computer historian, Allan George Bromley, Wright devised an apparatus to adapt standard X-ray equipment for linear tomography, or body section radiographs.[27] This process took several years to complete, but by early 1994, the duo had produced some 700 exposures that successfully separated out the individual layers of the mechanism. Wright, however, as the junior partner of the enterprise, was frustrated by the fact that Bromley returned to Sydney with the entire haul of images, leaving him, who had designed and built the imaging equipment to return to London empty handed, to nurse considerable spleen.

Bromley, however, fell victim to the onset of Hodgkin's Lymphoma, dying soon afterwards, after which Wright was able to retrieve the entire collection of images and return them to London where he set about the business of decoding and reconstructing the mechanism. Like Derek Price before him, however, the sequences of Wright's work on the Antikythera mechanism are so exhaustive and detailed that they hardly bear reproduction in this narrative, other than perhaps to say that Wright was quickly able to prove, somewhat to his satisfaction, that Price's reconstruction had indeed been fundamentally flawed.[28]

He did, however, advance on Price's original suggestion that the mechanism might have served as a complex planetarium, although his version took into account not only the motion of the Sun and Moon, but also the Inferior Planets (Mercury and Venus), and the Superior Planets (Mars,

[25] Wright, MT. *The Antikythera Mechanism Reconsidered*, Centre for the History of Science, Technology and Medicine, Imperial College London, London SW7 2AZ, UK

[26] Marchant, Jo (2009-02-10). *Decoding the Heavens: A 2,000-Year-Old Computer and the Century-long Search to Discover Its Secrets* (p. 169). Da Capo Press. Kindle Edition.

[27] Note: *Tomography* - a technique for displaying a representation of a cross section through a human body or other solid object using X-rays or ultrasound.

[28] Note: For a detailed overview of Wrights work, see Wright, MT. *The Antikythera Mechanism Reconsidered*, Centre for the History of Science, Technology and Medicine, Imperial College London, London SW7 2AZ, UK

Jupiter and Saturn). Wright worked on the basic supposition that the mechanism most likely mapped the movements of the sun and moon in accordance with the theories of Hipparchus, and that the five known planets listed above moved according to the simple epicyclic theory suggested by the theorem of Apollonios.[29]

Could it be possible, Wright asked himself, that the Antikythera mechanism included some arrangement of epicycle gearing to accommodate the anomalous motions of some or all of the planets? Inscriptions that Price had noted, but which he had later ignored, made mention of Venus, and the stationary points at which the planets appeared to stop, and then change direction. To prove that it was possible, Wright set about building a working model of such a planetarium by means of technology evident in the mechanism. Using the nameplate from an office door and a kicking plate salvaged from a pub, and armed with files, a hammer, and a chisel, and little else, he set to work.[30]

Wright's Epicycle Gear Arrangement | Basic Pin and Slot Gear System

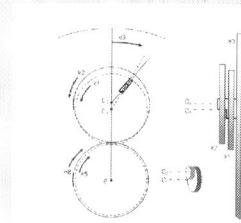

The first thing that Wright did was advance on Price's overall gear count, adding 4 gearwheels to create a total of 31, including one in Fragment C that he eventually identified as part of a Moon phase display. In a leap of logic not altogether dissimilar to Price, he created and displayed the phases of the moon by the rotation of a half black and half silvered ball, realized by the differential rotation of the sidereal cycle of the moon and the sun's yearly cycle. He also obtained

[29] Note: *In the Hipparchian* and *Ptolemaic* systems of astronomy, the epicycle (literally: on the circle in Greek) was a geometric model used to explain the variations in speed and direction of the apparent motion of the Moon, Sun, and planets. In particular, it explained the apparent retrograde motion of the five planets known at the time. Secondarily, it also explained changes in the apparent distances of the planets from Earth. *Apollonius* introduced an alternative epicyclic model, in which the planet turns about a point that itself orbits in a circle (the *deferent*) centered at or near the Earth. This epicyclic model is geometrically equivalent to an eccentric. Such models were well adapted for explaining other phenomena of planetary motion. For instance, if the Earth is displaced from the centre of a circular orbit, the orbiting body will appear to vary in speed (appearing faster when nearer the observer, slower when farther away), as is in fact observed for the Sun, Moon, and planets. By varying the relative sizes and rotation rates of the epicycle and deferent, in combination with the eccentric, a *flexible device may be obtained* for representing planetary motion. **Wilbur R. Knorr,** Professor of the History of Science, Stanford University, California. Author of Ancient Tradition of Geometric problems and others.

[30] Note: He did, however, have the advantage of computerized imagery and image enhancement software, which, of course, the ancient Greeks did not.

more accurate tooth counts (more in agreement with Price's original count) which facilitated a new gearing scheme, allowing him to concur at least with Price's theory that the upper back dial had been intended to display the Metonic cycle, with divisions over a five-turn scale indicating 235 lunar months (19 years, or 235 Synodic Months).

Then, measuring the dials at the back, Wright was struck by an epiphany. He realized that the main back dials were not in fact concentric circles at all, but a single spiral linking the two dials, with the upper a five-turn spiral, and by measuring the marks on it, he was able to calculate that each revolution of the pointer represented 47 divisions, making 235 in all. From this, he determined that the upper spiral must have displayed the 235 months of the Metonic 19-year cycle, as calculated by the gear train under the front dial. He also observed that fragmentary inscriptions on the subsidiary dial suggested that the pointer showed a count of four cycles of the 19-year period, equal to the 76-year Callippic cycle.[31] In further tentative leaps of faith and logic, he added that the lower back dial counted Draconic, or lunar months, and could perhaps have been used for eclipse prediction.

All of this was singularly brilliant, and the opus of a man without much in the way of academic credentials, reinforced with enormous gumption and self-belief. Echoing some of the lapses that he attributed to Derek Price, however, when he was unable to reconcile all of the known gears into a single coherent mechanism, he advanced the theory that the mechanism had been altered, or modified in some way, with some astronomical functions removed and others added. He had, after all, used various items of second hand detritus lying around his own workshop to build the replica, so it made sense that an ancient craftsman would have done likewise to build the original. In general, however, the brilliance of his work is unassailable, with perhaps his greatest stroke of genius being the incorporation of an epicyclic pin and slot engagement gear to simulate the elliptical anomaly in the angular velocity of the moon.[32]

---

[31] *Callippic cycle* is a particular approximate common multiple of the year (specifically the tropical year) and the synodic month that was proposed by Callippus during 330 BCE. It is a period of 76 years, as an improvement of the 19-year Metonic cycle.
[32] Michael Wrights own detailed explanation of this theory is contained in his two definitive papers, *Epicyclic Gearing and the Antikythera Mechanism, Parts I & II*

Front Face of Wright's Replica   Rear Face of Wright's Replica

On 6 March 2007, Michael Wright presented his findings and his completed replica to the National Hellenic Research Foundation in Athens, and although his work represented the greatest advance so far, and a brilliant piece of archaeological detective work, it was nonetheless incomplete. At the last minute, Wright had been forced to hurry his work against the sudden appearance of very stiff competition.

His contribution to the Antikythera saga thus far had been no less characterized by the egotism and professional rivalry than the work of Derek Price before him, but he had also never enjoyed the soaring academic credentials of his predecessor, and nor the funding and gravitas of Allan Bromley. He had conducted his research on his own time, within the constraints of employment and paid for largely out of his own pocket. After this heroic and largely unsung effort, however, Wright was stung deeply, almost at the moment of triumph, to discover that a high profile, academically supported and well-funded research project was bearing down on his very conclusions.

The Antikythera Research Project

The Antikythera Mechanism Research Project was born sometime in 1998, under the midwifery of a British mathematician and filmmaker by the name of Tony Freeth. Freeth had by then established a modest reputation in the documentary field, which allowed him to deploy a degree of professional influence that, in combination with a natural persuasiveness and an apparent inability to accept defeat, offered him a considerable advantage over the amateur efforts of Michael Wright. Freeth also had the advantage of technology, in particular computer and imaging technology, a considerable advance over Wright's homemade tomographic apparatus.

The story, as it is told by Freeth himself, is that he happened to be glancing through an edition of the science journal Nature, and was struck by a series of images (of a goldfish and a grasshopper) taken using a revolutionary new system of tomographic x-rays (*400kV microfocus Computed Tomography System*) then under development. Freeth sensed that this might be the key to unlocking the inner mystery of the Antikythera mechanism, and he made contact with a small, specialized imaging company located in Hertfordshire, England, responsible for developing the technology, and with very little persuasion, X-Tek agreed to come on board.

Next, the Hewlett-Packard labs in Palo Alto were persuaded to release a young researcher by the name of Tom Malzbender, who had developed a unique lighting and imaging system to enhance the readability of ancient cuneiform tablets. The essence of this approach was a lighting dome fitted with up to fifty flash bulbs positioned to illuminate any subject from multiple different angles, which, in combination with imaging enhancing computer software, promised to expose the texts and inscriptions on the device to a degree that Price could only have dreamed.

The greatest obstacle, however, proved to be the Greeks themselves, primarily because of the long simmering debate over the return of the Elgin Marbles at that time. The campaign for the return of these artifacts to Greece has tended to ebb and wane with the political climate, but in the run-up to the 2004 Olympics, a strong movement advocating a return tended to translate into considerable anti-British feeling. This found convenient expression in a blunt refusal by the museum staff in Athens to allow Freeth or any of his team access to the mechanism.

Seconding a handful of Greek academics, however, Freeth went straight to the source by petitioning the Greek Ministry of Culture, which proved, after much effort, to be successful. In September 2005, the Antikythera Research Project team finally gained access to the fragments.

Then, as if to add to Michael Wright's gathering sense of blighted fortune, the museum official, gathering up the fragments in preparation for study, unearthed a previously undiscovered fragment. This proved to be the bottom right hand corner of the second dial positioned on the rear of the device, which had caused immense head scratching for both Wright and Price, and which, had it been discovered earlier, would have helped at least Wright's quest enormously.

However, battling against his own technical and logistical hurdles, Freeth and the X-Tek team worked to complete construction of a custom imaging cubicle against a looming deadline. As this work was underway, the Hewlett-Packard team arrived in Athens and went to work. Ultimately, some 4,000 images of 82 separate fragments were created, which, with help of a certain amount of computerized manipulation, produced stunning results. Over 2,000 inscribed characters out of a potential 20,000 were revealed, improving enormously over the 800 or so that Price and Wright had been able to identify and decipher.[33]

In the meanwhile, when the bulky imaging equipment finally arrived in Athens, and was put to work, thousands of high-resolution images were produced that revealed the internal topography

[33] Marchant, Jo (2009-02-10). Decoding the Heavens: A 2,000-Year-Old Computer--and the Century-long Search to Discover Its Secrets (p. 244). Da Capo Press. Kindle Edition.

of the mechanism in a manner that exceeded all expectations. Aiding this spectacular result was the fact that very little intact bronze remained within the fragments, allowing for clearer CT penetration and imaging, and a much finer array of detail than could ever have been realistically been expected.

Thus, as Wright battled in his home workshop to perfect and complete his replica, Freeth set about decoding the huge volume of digital information that he now had access to. In the first instance, the various inscriptions were analyzed with initial results that would have gratified the irritated Wright considerably. Identified on the back of the mechanism, near the top, was the Greek word EΛIKI, meaning spiral. This confirmed Wright's key assertion that the series of concentric circles visible on the back dial were in fact a single spiral. This fact, incidentally, was also confirmed by the lost fragment that, under CT imaging, revealed that the two black dials did indeed comprise of a single spiral. Likewise, it was now clear that this spiral was divided into the 235 synodic months of the 19-year lunisolar cycle. Therefore, while the front dial indicated the day of the year, it was evident now that the back dial tracked months and years over a much longer period.

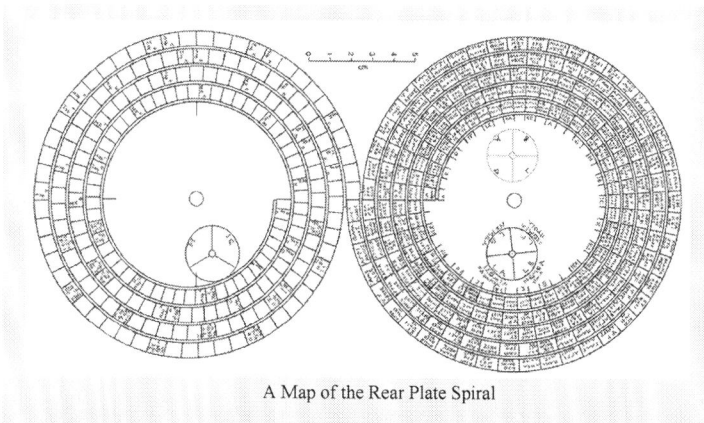

A Map of the Rear Plate Spiral

On the front dial, adding to Price's observation of the zodiac signs Virgo and Libra, could now be read Scorpio, confirming that the zodiac scale ran clockwise around the front dial. On the front door plate, meanwhile, was discovered reference to the planets Venus and Mercury, and the "Stationary Points," with numbers possibly relating to the distances between the planets and the sun.[34] In addition to all of this, a long list of operating instructions discovered on the back of the mechanism suggested that the device had not been intended to be used by the individual who

[34] Greek Philosopher Aristotle (384 – 322 BCE) was the first to adopt the concept of a spherical Earth surrounded by a heavenly realm, with separate circles or spheres carrying round the Sun, Moon, five planets and the stars, which were all fixed in place on their sphere.

conceived and constructed it, but rather by a wealthy layperson with a very general interest.

However, the question of the ultimate function of the device remained a mystery, and while inscriptions and general text advanced the quest, ultimately, the answer still lay in a combination of mathematics and mechanics. Freeth, therefore, took his turn to lock himself away in a quiet room in order to pore over this vast haul of enhanced imagery.

For want of any proof to the contrary, Freeth accepted Wright's assertion that the gearing on the front of the device modeled the movements of the planets as well as anomalies in the speed of the sun and the moon, a theory supported by new inscriptions now decoded. The role of the two dials at the rear of the mechanism, however, remained obscure, and it was to this that Freeth applied his considerable intellect.

His first discovery was how the upper spiral reading on the back facia was displayed. Wright's suggestion had been that beads or markers of some sort might have been moved around the spirals to indicate specific dates. Freeth, however, concluded from a surviving pointer that in fact an extending arm with a pin at the end travelled around the spiral groove in a manner not unlike a stylus on a vinyl record, taking the requisite 19-years to complete its cycle, at which point it could be reset by hand.

In the matter of the lower spiral, Freeth had the advantage of the missing fragment to work with, which now revealed parts of all the rings with their specific scale divisions. Inscribed into the segments on this scale could clearly be identified 16 blocks of characters, or "glyphs" as they were described, at intervals of one, five, and six months. A few of these glyphs contained the character "Σ," and some an "H," with some containing both. There was also what appeared to be an anchor sign, followed by a number, and then one more letter at the bottom. Price had noticed a few of these, but the remainder, until that point, had been unclear. As far as Freeth could determine, this all pointed towards the fact that this particular dial was an eclipse predictor.

The various mathematics and mechanical permutations that led to this conclusion lie somewhat beyond the scope of this narrative, but suffice to say that a brilliant feat of archaeological detective work had been undertaken, the details of which are available from a number of sources.[35] Freeth's conclusion, however, where Price had presented the device as a calendar computer, and Wright a planetarium, was that this device was both, but is fundamental role was that of an eclipse predictor.

This, however, presupposes a requirement for the ancient Greeks to know and understand the cycles of lunar and solar eclipses, which, if true, removes the device somewhat from the realm of science to that of ritual and religion. The ancient Greeks did indeed place great significance on the cycles of the sun and the moon, and across the ancient world, eclipses, and in particular lunar eclipses, were of great connotation.

The very word eclipse comes from the ancient Greek ekleipsis, meaning abandoned,

---

[35] Note: detailed descriptions of the work of **Tony Freeth** in this regard, along with *Bitsakis Y., Moussas X., Seiradakis J. H., Tselikas A., Mangou H., Zafeiropoulou M., Hadland R., Bate D., Ramsey A., Allen M., Crawley A., Hockley P., Malzbender T., Gelb D, Ambrisco W., Edmunds M. G., Jones A., Steele J. M.,* are easily obtainable online under the headings: ***Eclipse prediction on the ancient Greek astronomical calculating machine known as the Antikythera Mechanism. Decoding an ancient computer. Calendars with Olympiad display and eclipse prediction on the Antikythera Mechanism. Decoding the ancient Greek astronomical calculator known as the Antikythera Mechanism.***

suggesting that a lunar or solar eclipse was a frown on the face of the Gods, and a harbinger of ill fortune. The ancient Greeks could trace their philosophical roots to the ancient Babylonians, for whom eclipses carried particular meaning. The Babylonians were the first to use the Saros cycle (relating to the lunar cycle of 223 months, corresponding to 223 divisions on the "spiral" that Freeth was able to determine with the aid of the lost fragment) to predict eclipses.

Freeth, therefore, felt certain that these Grecian gears had been used primarily to determine the time and date of lunar and solar eclipses. If so, this presented the same anomalous gearing requirements that Wright had identified, meaning that the device not only modeled circular motion, but elliptical motion too, and moreover, a precessing ellipse. Again, if true, this implies a staggering degree of mathematical, mechanical and astronomical virtuosity. Price had taken a leap of faith by proposing a differential gear, but more elegant still was the pin and slot system proposed by Wright, and now proven by Freeth. This ingenious solution, unrecorded in any ancient astronomical literature, creates a non-uniform circular motion equivalent in angle (but not in spatial motion in depth) to the standard deferent-plus-epicycle lunar theory.[36]

And so the long journey of understanding the philosophy and reason behind the Antikythera mechanism reached its conclusion. Upon this note of mechanical, mathematical and philosophical mastery, however, it would seem fair to conclude by dwelling for a moment on a more human scale of the enterprise.

The brilliant work undertaken by Derek John de Solla Price – a lifetime, no less, dedicated to understanding the message encoded in this and similar devices – was spoiled at the last minute by professional arrogance and a certain over-familiarity with the protocols of empiricism and logic embedded in the scientific ethos.

"As far as I am concerned," he wrote to a friend and colleague upon the conclusion of his investigation, "[this] wraps the whole thing up."[37]

Wraps the whole thing up? Hardly so!

Wright, in his inexpert and frustrated way, was able to advance the quest far beyond Price's rather self-satisfied conclusion, only to find, as he neared his own conclusion, that the resource rich juggernaut of Tony Freeth was bearing down on his stern and threatening to eclipse his achievements at the last moment. Indeed, Tony Freeth published his findings in the prestigious scientific journal Nature, while Wright had to be content with clockwork periodicals which relatively nobody but oddballs such as he were ever apt to read.

With his stunning findings, Tony Freeth addressed an audience in Athens in an auditorium packed to the rafters with enthusiasts, all gasping as the beauty of his theories and the magnificence of his work. In the audience, however, seething in righteous indignation, sat Michael Wright. When it came his turn to take the podium, he did so, according to another

---

[36] On the Pin-and-Slot Device if the Antikythera Mechanism, With a new Application to the Superior Planets – CHRISTIAN C. CARMAN, Universidad Nacional de Quilmes/CONICET, ALAN THORNDIKE, University of Puget Sound, and JAMES EVANS, University of Puget Sound.

[37] Marchant, Jo (2009-02-10). Decoding the Heavens: A 2,000-Year-Old Computer--and the Century-long Search to Discover Its Secrets (p. 256). Da Capo Press. Kindle Edition.

speaker, in half an hour of continuously controlled rage.[38] Detailing the manifold difficulties that he had confronted and overcome in his quest to find the answer so elegantly placed before the audience by his competitor, Wright made his claims, illuminated his contribution and confirmed that he was still very much in the picture, and still had more to say.

Michael T. Wright and his Antikythera Mechanism Replica

All sides, however, reconciled in the production of a BBCE documentary detailing the Tony Freeth version of the tale, but also saluting Wright's brilliance in identifying and incorporating the pin-and-slot mechanism as a solution to the irregularities of the lunar ellipse, and other aspects of his work and contributions to the conclusions that were by then widely accepted.

Therefore, more than a century after the device had been lifted from the floor of the Ionian Sea, it can claim to be understood, and generally decoded. The hand that created this extraordinary device would most certainly have belonged to an ancient intellect of staggering brilliance, searching, as we all do, for an understanding of the cosmos. The pointers on the front of the casing indicated the changing positions of the sun, the moon and the planets in the Zodiac, with the additional indication of the date and the phases of the moon, while the spiral dials at the back indicated the month and the year according to the combined lunar/solar calendar, ultimately predicting the timing of the eclipses.

Research, however, has not ceased. It continues under the aegis of the Antikythera Mechanism Research Project, a program underwritten by a variety of funders, and including academics and researchers from various parts of the world. The Project, however, is now primarily a database and a source of material for the further study of the phenomenon, and no longer a quest for fresh theories regarding the origins, age and function of the device.

And that, indeed, in the words of Derek Price, would appear to wrap the matter up!

---

[38] Lake, Ed. *Ed Lake uncovers the story of the Antikythera mechanism, a 2,000-year old piece of clockwork*, The Telegraph, 08 Jan 2009.

Online Resources

Other books about ancient history by Charles River Editors

Other books about ancient Greece by Charles River Editors

Other books about the Antikythera Mechanism on Amazon

Other books about the Phaistos Disc on Amazon

Further Reading

Anthony, David W. 2007. *The Horse, the Wheel, and Language: How Bronze-Age Riders from the Eurasian Steppes Shaped the Modern World*. Princeton, New Jersey: Princeton University Press.

Bowden, E. 1992. *Cybele the Axe-Goddess: Alliterative Verse, Linear B Relationships and Cult Ritual of the Phaistos Disc*. Amsterdam: Gieben.

Callender, Gae. "The Middle Kingdom Renaissance (c. 2055-1650 BCE)." In *The Oxford History of Ancient Egypt*, edited by Ian Shaw, 148-183. Oxford: Oxford University Press.

Cate, Arie ten. 2011. "Patterns on an Ancient Artifact: A Coincidence?" *Statistica Neerlandica* 65: 116-124.

Davis, S. 1970. *The Decipherment of the Minoan Linear A and Pictographic Scripts*. Johannesburg: Witwatersrand University Press.

Diodorus Siculus. *The Library of History*. Translated by C.H. Oldfather. Cambridge,

Massachusetts: Harvard University Press, 2004.

Duhoux, Yves. 2000. "How Not to Decipher the Phaistos Disc: A Review Article." *American Journal of Archaeology* 104: 597-600.

Faulkner, Richard O. *The Ancient Egyptian Pyramid Texts*. Stilwell, Kansas: Digireads.com Publishing, 2007.

James, Peter; Thorpe, Nick (1995). Ancient Inventions. New York: Ballantine. ISBN 0-345-40102-6.

Herodotus. 2003. *The Histories*. Translated by Aubrey de Sélincourt. London: Penguin Books.

Kuhrt, Amélie. 2010. *The Ancient Near East: c. 3000-330 BCE*. 2 vols. London: Routledge.

Macqueen, J.G. 2003. *The Hittites and Their Contemporaries in Asia Minor*. London: Thames and Hudson.

Marchant, Jo (6 November 2008). Decoding the Heavens: Solving the Mystery of the World's First Computer. William Heinemann Ltd. ISBN 0-434-01835-X.

Morritt, Robert D. 2010. *Stones that Speak*. Newcastle upon Tyne, United Kingdom: Cambridge   Scholars Publishing.

Muenzer, Paul J. 1985. "The Phaistos Disc Deciphered." *Midwest Quarterly* 26: 271-280.

Pomerance, Leon. 1976. *The Phaistos Disc: An Interpretation of Astronomical Symbols*. Göteborg: Paul Aströms.

Preziosi, Donald and Louise A. Hitchcock. 1999. *Aegean Art and Architecture*. Oxford: Oxford University Press.

Rosheim, Mark E. (1994). Robot Evolution: The Development of Anthrobotics. John Wiley & Sons. ISBN 0-471-02622-0.

Russo, Lucio (2004). The Forgotten Revolution: How Science Was Born in 300 BCE and Why It Had To Be Reborn. Berlin: Springer. ISBN 3-540-20396-6.

Schwartz, Benjamin. 1959. "The Phaistos Disc." *Journal of Near Eastern Studies*. 18: 105-112.

————. 1959b. "The Phaistos Disc II." *Journal of Near Eastern Studies*. 18: 222-226.

Strabo. *Geography*. Translated by Horace Leonard Jones. Cambridge, Massachusetts: Harvard University Press, 2001.

Steele, J. M. (2000). Observations and Predictions of Eclipse Times by Early Astronomers. Dordrecht: Kluwer Academic. ISBN 0-7923-6298-5.

Stephenson, F. R. (1997). Historical Eclipses and the Earth's Rotation. Cambridge, UK: Cambridge Univ. Press. ISBN 0-521-46194-4.

Toomer, G. J. (1998). Ptolemy's Almagest. Translated by Toomer, G. J. Princeton, New Jersey: Princeton Univ. Press.

Whittaker, H. 2005. "Social and Symbolic Aspects of Minoan Writing." *European Journal of Archaeology* 8: 29-41.

Free Books by Charles River Editors

We have brand new titles available for free most days of the week. To see which of our titles are currently free, click on this link.

Discounted Books by Charles River Editors

We have titles at a discount price of just 99 cents everyday. To see which of our titles are currently 99 cents, click on this link.

Printed in Great Britain
by Amazon

85109489R00041